CAS Paper 36

Management of regulation in the food chain - balancing costs, benefits and effects

Proceedings of a conference organised by the Centre for Agricultural Strategy, held at The Royal Society, 6 Carlton House Terrace, London SW1Y 5AG on 11 February 1997

Edited by B J Marshall & F A Miller

Centre for Agricultural Strategy
University of Reading
PO Box 236
Earley Gate
Reading RG6 6AT

June 1997

ISBN 0 7049 1133 7

ISSN 0141 1330

Printed by TA Printers, 43-45 Milford Road, Reading RG1 8LG

Originally established by the Nuffield Foundation in 1975, the **Centre for Agricultural Strategy** is a self-financing unit within the Faculty of Agriculture and Food at the University of Reading.

Acknowledgements

The Centre gratefully acknowledges the support and advice provided by the following organisations:

Ministry of Agriculture, Fisheries and Food

AgrEvo UK Crop Protection Ltd

Campden & Chorleywood Food Research Association

Dalgety Food Technology Centre

DowElanco Europe Ltd

European Food Law Association of the UK

Food and Drink Federation

Institute of Food Research

Law Laboratories Ltd

Northern Foods plc

SAINSBURY'S J Sainsbury plc

Unigate plc

Unilever Research Laboratory

ZENECA Zeneca Agrochemicals

ZENECA Zeneca Plant Sciences

Contents

Abbreviations and Acronyms

ACC	Association of County Councils
ACNFP	Advisory Committee on Novel Foods and Processes
ACRE	Advisory Committee on Releases to the Environment
ADC	Association of District Councils
AMA	Association of Metropolitan Authorities
BSE	Bovine Spongiform Encephalopathy
CA	Consumers' Association
CAP	Common Agricultural Policy
CAS	Centre for Agricultural Strategy
CJD	Creutzfeld-Jacob Disease
DTI	Department of Trade and Industry
DU	Deregulation Unit
EC	European Commission
EEC	European Economic Community
EFLA/UK	European Food Law Association of the United Kingdom
EHO	Environmental Health Officer
EU	European Union
EUROPMI	European Small Business Organisation
FDA	Food and Drugs Administration
FDF	Food and Drink Federation
GATT	General Agreement on Tariffs and Trade
HACCP	Hazard Analysis and Critical Control Points
HMSO	Her Majesty's Stationery Office
HSE	Health and Safety Executive
IACS	Integrated Administration and Control System
ITSA	Institute of Trading Standards Associations
LACOTS	Local Authorities Coordinating Body on Food and Trading Standards
LGA	Local Government Association
MAFF	Ministry of Agriculture, Fisheries and Food
MP	Member of Parliament
NCC	National Consumer Council
NFU	National Farmers' Union

OECD	Organisation for Economic Cooperation and Development
plc	Public Liability Company
PPC	Public Protection Committee
QUID	Quantitative Ingredient Determination
SAFE	Sustainable Agriculture, Food and Environment
SCF	Scientific Committee on Foods
SEAC	Spongiform Encephalopathies Advisory Committee
SLIM	Simpler Legislation in the Internal Market
UK	United Kingdom
US	United States
USA	United States of America
VTEC	Verocytotoxin-producing strain of *Escherichia coli*
WTO	World Trade Organisation

Marshall BJ & Miller FA (Eds)(1997) *Management of regulation in the food chain - balancing costs, benefits and effects.*
CAS Paper 36. Reading: Centre for Agricultural Strategy.

Preface

This conference was well timed. Questions about the regulation of the food industry are currently the subject of a great deal of media attention. In the light of recent food scares consumer groups, as well as other food industry representative organisations have questioned the adequacy of existing institutional arrangements. Some have called for a radical reallocation of responsibilities. The industry itself is deeply concerned both about the cost and effectiveness of regulations and about their impact on its competitiveness. For both, the restoration of confidence in the United Kingdom (UK) food regulatory regime is critical.

The Centre for Agricultural Strategy, one of whose functions is to promote informed debate on issues of long-run significance sought, through this conference, to bring together the interests involved. The intention was to understand the position of each group and to consider options for the organisation of food law, administration and enforcement. All sectors were invited to comment on the report of the Food, Drink and Agriculture Task Force (1993), to review the Government's deregulation initiative and to take account of the review of food law currently being undertaken by the European Commission (EC). The Task Force had stressed the highly regulated nature of the food industry. The Government's deregulation policy was designed to minimise burdens on industry whilst ensuring adequate consumer protection. The EC seeks coherence in Community food legislation and wishes to explore the scope for simplification and rationalisation. In the light of their comments on the current situation, contributors were invited to consider what organisational changes, if any, were needed to restore public confidence in the safety of food.

The papers in this report set out the authoritative views of representatives of key sectors of the industry and of consumers.

The publication also includes a record of the well-informed debate which followed and supplemented the material in the papers. Together they provide an accessible and informed account of the current debate about food safety regulation. As such they contribute both to public understanding and to the work of food policy makers and their legal advisers in the UK and the European Union.

The Centre for Agricultural Strategy is grateful to the many food companies and associated organisations who provided support and sponsorship. Without them we could not have promoted this event. We appreciated, too, and are encouraged by, the large number of participants from these diverse industries and interest groups, who played so positive a part in ensuring a lively and productive debate on these issues which are sensitive, controversial and important.

J S Marsh
Director
Centre for Agricultural Strategy

Marshall BJ & Miller FA (Eds)(1997) *Management of regulation in the food chain - balancing costs, benefits and effects.*
CAS Paper 36. Reading: Centre for Agricultural Strategy.

Opening Address

Angela Browning, MP

INTRODUCTION

I am delighted to be here today, and to have the opportunity to open this Conference. The Centre for Agricultural Strategy has a well deserved reputation for the quality of its Conferences and this one has all the hallmarks of another highly successful event. You have a most interesting programme before you and some first-rate speakers. It is particularly topical to be looking at some of the issues you are considering today in the light of our recent announcement of our intention to create a new Food Safety Council, chaired by an independent Food Safety Adviser. I shall say more about this in a moment.

IMPORTANCE OF CONSUMER PROTECTION

When considering food legislation, the government regards protection of consumers as of paramount importance. Food laws are necessary - *essential* - to protect the public. We need to ensure that food is safe; that consumers are not cheated; and that they have the essential information needed to make choices relating to health and nutrition. We must do nothing which jeopardises this important protection. It is not a case of 'them' and 'us'; of 'industry' and 'consumers' and 'ne'er the twain shall meet'. Every one of us in this room - whatever our background and interests - is a consumer. We all have a key and overriding interest in ensuring that the food we, and our families, eat is safe.

KEY FACTS AND FIGURES

The food chain is of the greatest importance to the economy of this country. The wealth generated by the sector accounts for around 9% of Gross Domestic Product. The 350 000 businesses in the sector provide 3.5 million jobs. And exports of food and drink are earning us £10 billion abroad.

SENSIBLE REGULATION AND DEREGULATION

While food safety and consumer protection are paramount, we need also to ensure that our food and drink industry is not bound up in unnecessary red tape. If the industry is to compete in a global economy it needs sensible food laws that assist fair competition and trade and strike out unnecessary barriers. Too much law, or bad law, imposes real burdens - particularly on small businesses. Companies need to concentrate on the key legislation, on the laws that have a real bearing on food safety and consumer protection. If they are snowed under by excessive, minor pieces of legislation they may lose sight of what really matters.

Deregulation has been, and remains, a key policy of this Government, and of the Ministry of Agriculture, Fisheries and Food (MAFF). I know that some people get nervous when the words 'deregulation' and 'MAFF' are used in close association. But let me emphasise that deregulation is *not* - emphatically *not* - about removing essential protection. It is, however, very much about removing the unnecessary burdens that add unwarranted costs to business and stifle growth of a competitive economy.

When we are considering any new regulation, or indeed removing old regulations, we have to strike the right balance between costs and benefits. How do we do this? First of all by a rigorous system of Regulatory Appraisal. Lucy Neville-Rolfe will be speaking about Regulatory Appraisal this afternoon. For now, let me just say that these appraisals set out the costs to business of the proposed legislation, and compare them with the benefits, using risk appraisal techniques. We also guard against any tendency to impose additional, unnecessary burdens, what we call 'gold plating'. Nor do we 'double bank' by duplicating existing laws. Again, just to keep Ministers on their toes, we now have to certify that a checklist for avoiding gold plating and double banking has been followed. All of this helps to ensure that we make new legislation prudently and wisely, to avoid the overregulation that has proved burdensome in the past.

CURRENT ISSUES

Done properly, deregulation is, therefore, a good thing. In line with our Food Law Deregulation Plan, last year we undertook substantial simplification and liberalisation of United Kingdom (UK) food law. A package of measures was introduced on 1 January 1996 which removed many unnecessary compositional requirements. Consolidation and review of the Food Labelling Regulations, completed on 1 July 1996, led to further deregulation of UK compositional regulations. The food industry now has a much shorter, and clearer, set of legislation which it has to follow.

In conjunction with the Department of Health, we have made an order under the Deregulation and Contracting Out Act 1994, to introduce new, business-friendly procedures to be followed when local authorities issue food safety improvement notices. This does not impede in any way an Environmental Health Officer's ability to take immediate enforcement action where the circumstances merit it.

As many of you will know, the European Commission is currently considering ways of consolidating and simplifying food hygiene legislation. One of the most important elements we strongly want to emerge from this consolidation is the affirmation that the operation of 'hazard analysis principles' is the system of choice when it comes to food safety controls. The Government recognises hazard analysis to be a fundamentally important tool in this area. It places clear responsibility on food businesses to manage their operations in a 'hands on', systematic and safe way. Hazard analysis provides a far greater assurance that safe food will be delivered than does reliance on prescriptive legislation which can serve to lull food business operators into a false sense of security. Furthermore, the requirement to operate 'hazard analysis principles' is a feature of some, but not all, product specific hygiene directives. We should like to see this requirement extended across the board. We also want to see the prescriptive provisions in hygiene directives reviewed with a view to retaining only those that can fully be justified in the interests of public safety.

FOOD SAFETY COUNCIL AND FOOD SAFETY ADVISER
If the public does not have confidence that the food they buy is safe, of good quality, and what it claims to be, no amount of elegant streamlining and deregulation is going to convince them otherwise. We have seen in the last year the major ramifications there can be for the agriculture and food industries when consumers lose confidence in the safety of food. That is why, as I have said earlier, we need to have adequate regulation to assure them that they are properly protected from food safety risks.

But we need to go further than this. We need to regain the trust of consumers; to reassure them that, in the process of balancing that I have talked about, their interests are given adequate weight; and we need to make sure that the decision making process is open and transparent. This is the thinking that lies behind our announcement, two weeks ago, of our intention to create a Food Safety Council, chaired by an independent, eminent adviser on food safety. The Council and the Adviser will provide the public with a source of independent advice, publicly given, which they will be able to trust. It will take a strategic view of the longer-term agenda on food policy matters, and draw together issues of importance ranging across the work of all our existing independent advisory committees. Its membership will be widely drawn, including all those with an interest in the safety of the food supply. The new Food Safety Council will therefore play an important part in ensuring that decisions on food safety are based on the best possible independent advice which takes account of all the interests.

Of course, some have argued that what we have proposed does not go far enough, that what is really needed is a food agency. But the proponents of an agency have not said exactly what sort of body it would be, or how it would work. They talk about separating off the consumer interest from the producer interest, but they fail to recognise that the food chain is an integrated whole, where decisions taken by the producer have important effects for the consumer and where safety must be paramount from start to finish; and notwithstanding what has happened with Bovine Spongiform Encephalopathy (BSE) in the last year, it is a trend that was already developing and one which I think, because of BSE, is rightly at the forefront of our thinking. For example, when talking to farmers, it is evident that they are increasingly recognising the importance for them, at the point of food production, of much more involvement in what is required at the end of the food chain - not just in terms of the quality of the produce itself but also of the transparency needed to enable the processors and retailers to give the necessary guarantees to consumers.

They also miss another important point - that any body which takes and implements decisions on food safety will then naturally defend those decisions. Our proposal is more imaginative than this. It separates out the functions, so that Ministers remain responsible for taking and implementing decisions, whilst the Food Safety Council and Adviser are able to stand back and take an independent, supervisory role. If they do not like what they see, they will have the power to criticise publicly, or in their reports. In effect, what we are proposing will make a real contribution to improving food safety, and will help to ensure that the quality of our regulation is good, without creating costly bureaucratic structures which would be out of touch with the important practicalities of operating in the food industry. Perhaps I could just reiterate that when Douglas Hogg made this announcement he emphasised that this is not a 'soft option' for Ministers. Quite rightly we have to stand at the despatch box and account to Parliament for the policy decisions that we make. In the case of food safety those policies are often based on advice given by independent committees, but the Food Safety Adviser will have an overarching authority and will be able to comment publicly on policy announcements; and Ministers will be put in a position where they have to defend their decisions.

PERORATION
I am conscious that time is moving on and you have a full day ahead of you. The Centre for Agricultural Strategy must be commended for producing such a highly relevant and topical programme, and for lining up such a distinguished selection of speakers. I am sure you will have an excellent and thought-provoking day. I am only sorry that I shall not be able to stay to hear your discussions. However, my colleague, MAFF's Deregulation Minister Tim Boswell has joined you and hopes to stay most of the morning. I am pleased to say that MAFF has been able, in a small way, to help support this conference. I wish you every success.

DISCUSSION
Mrs Vera Chaney (Green Network) stressed the importance of including professional medical expertise, preferably a pathologist, in the membership of the Food Safety Council.

Mrs Angela Browning gave an assurance that there will be medical representation and noted the preference for a pathologist. She also confirmed the important new development under which the Chief Medical Adviser will be officially advising MAFF as well as the Department of Health, and will as part of his duty of safeguarding the public's interests communicate his views on food safety issues.

Mr David Gaunt (British Simmental Cattle Society) said that it is generally recognised that discipline begins in the home and he asked the Minister to comment on whether MAFF undertakes discussions with the Department for Education with regard to teaching food hygiene in the home. He also felt that the title 'Food Safety Council' implies another bureaucratic layer and suggested that 'Food Authority' would be more appropriate; and asked whether the new body would have authority independent of government.

Mrs Browning fully accepted the point about the importance of safety in the home and recognised that a lot of problems such as food poisoning could be avoided with proper handling and cooking of food, right the way through the chain, but importantly in the home. She drew attention to the MAFF 'Food Sense' literature which is widely disseminated to a range of institutions, including schools, and confirmed that relevant discussions do take place with colleagues in the Department for Education, not only about food hygiene but also about the nutrition aspects. On the question of the independence of the new body, Mrs Browning explained the difficulties, especially in relation to a loss of public confidence, of Ministers setting out their policies based on expert committee advice on the one hand, and the expression of alternative opinions by other experienced and qualified authorities. She therefore felt that the appointment of a Food Safety Adviser, backed by the expert team of Council members, with the responsibility of assessing whether the government has got it right, has not gone far enough, or even got it wrong, is the most effective way of ensuring the appropriate degree of independence. Furthermore the Council secretariat, which is now being discussed with the organisations concerned, will not be based in MAFF nor in the Department of Health, and will therefore be seen to be transparently independent.

Mrs Teresa Wickham (CAS and Food Industry Consultant) referred to the proposal to set up a Food Safety Council and asked whether consideration is being given to its interface with a possible European Union (EU) Food Agency.

Mrs Browning confirmed that the EU is looking at setting up such a body and expressed expectation that they would have regular contact, because so much of our food law is now based on EU-wide regulation. She felt that within the single market it is vitally important that UK regulations are as compatible as possible with EU regulations, that the interface between the EC and member governments should be effective, that their agenda will be published in advance for full public information purposes and that the outcome of their meetings will also be published.

Marshall BJ & Miller FA (Eds)(1997) *Management of regulation in the food chain - balancing costs, benefits and effects.* CAS Paper 36. Reading: Centre for Agricultural Strategy.

1 Making and enforcing food chain regulations - the factors that determine when, by whom, and how

John S Marsh

INTRODUCTION

Those of us who grew up in families are familiar with the cry 'Daddy, tell him to give me a turn!' When other people's behaviour conflicts with our own interests or preferences we may resort to 'higher authority' to attain our goals. This is rational. It is likely to be both more effective and less costly than seeking to impose our will by sheer force. To an important degree, life in communities depends upon mutual acceptance and the perceived effectiveness of 'higher authorities'. Where their views are expressed not just on an *ad hoc* basis but as judgements which are generally applicable, we have 'regulations'.

This conference takes as its starting point the report of the Food, Drink and Agriculture Task Force (1993) and the more recent report of the Deregulation Task Force (1995). Both saw overregulation as an issue for the food industry. Both recognised that to serve society satisfactorily the industries which comprise the human food chain need regulation as well as freedom to respond to market forces. The papers that follow will explore concerns about both the legitimacy and the effectiveness of our present system of regulation and the case for changes in its organisational structure. This paper seeks to identify areas in which we feel there is a need for regulation. It also draws attention to some of the limitations of a regulatory approach.

WHY REGULATE?
Market failures

Markets alone do not take account of the full economic impact of the activities of industries, including those in the food chain, on the use of resources. In terms of economic jargon, they neglect 'public goods', such as the impact on the environment, and 'externalities', the benefits or costs which the activities of one business impose on individuals or other businesses.

The out-of-town hypermarket provides a good example. It provides a huge range of alternative products under one roof saving both time and discomfort for the shopper. It can also provide a focal point for charity collectors, whose activities do not figure in the accounts of the shop but who clearly provide a service which some people value. It can ease congestion in city streets by providing adequate parking facilities, but it adds to traffic problems in suburban areas. It may generate new business for those who supply transport or service motor cars but it is likely to reduce the business of other food retailers in the vicinity. If the possibility of regulatory intervention did not exist, none of these economic benefits and costs need figure in the business appraisal of those who invest in the hypermarket.

Food safety

Markets will certainly punish food businesses which are seen to have supplied unsafe food. However, if failures in safety are not detected or attributed to the right source, markets will not penalise the defaulter. Given the plurality of possible causes of stomach upsets, the source of relatively minor failures of food hygiene may not be identified. As a result, bad practice can continue unchecked. Where a serious failure is recognised, the response of markets may be disproportionate and misdirected. For example, as producers of yoghurt will remember, where an unsafe product sold by a single manufacturer can result in a collapse in the market for all businesses who produce similar goods.

Regulations, which are seen to be effective in ensuring safety and detecting any lapses in standards, safeguard the industry as well as the consumer. Confidence in regulatory systems is essential but is difficult to achieve and is easily undermined. Changing systems of food production and distribution and changing methods of domestic food storage and use mean that approaches which traditionally have been adequate fail to meet current needs. New scientific discoveries and the ever increasing ability of instruments to detect small quantities of undesirable materials mean that any existing set of rules is likely to become outdated. Where a particular problem or perception of a need for updating is said to demonstrate the failure of the system as a whole, confidence may be destroyed in quite unrelated areas. Casual attacks on the probity of the system help neither the industry nor the consumer.

Reliable information

To make informed decisions consumers need accurate information, in terms they can understand, about the quality and many other characteristics of products offered for sale as well as their price. The range of relevant information is substantial. It involves not only the chemical composition of the food product but also its nutritional characteristics. Increasingly, there have been demands for information about how food is produced: is it 'organic'?; is it welfare friendly?; does it damage the environment? Consumers who have specific ethical or religious priorities may need to know how animals were slaughtered or whether the products contain material from particular species. Vegetarians need to know that the 'vegetarian meals' on offer contain no animal ingredients.

It is impracticable, if not impossible, for individual consumers to check all such claims. The increasing number of highly processed manufactured food products make traditional checks for freshness and wholesomeness inapplicable. Some of the language used in selling food is imprecise - for example some products are described as 'natural' - but is there really a market for 'unnatural' or 'supernatural' products? There is a serious possibility that the information provided will be inaccurate or misleading.

Regulations designed to ensure that information is understandable and accurate have a long history in food legislation. Rules relating to weights and measures and adulteration help to prevent consumers from being cheated by unscrupulous traders. However, claims relating to the complex products are not so simply checked. Rules about temperatures and hygiene in food preparation establishments can prevent some problems. Minimum labelling requirements may provide consumers with much of the information they need. To be effective, however, the rules have to be enforced and the information provided relevant and understood.

Minority concerns

One mark of a civilised society is how it looks after its weakest members. In the food industry this has to include provision for those who have special food needs or allergic reactions to products which cause no problem to the generality of humanity. It also encompasses problems of access to shopping facilities and the provision of appropriate trolleys, toilets, etc. Such provision, and the identification of products which may have an allergic effect, involves cost and is unlikely to attract a substantial volume of business. From a profit-maximising viewpoint it is unattractive. Most major food companies recognise that they have a responsibility to meet such needs and do so willingly. However, for issues such as access and the adequacy of labelling of some ingredients which may threaten the health of some vulnerable individuals, regulations are used to safeguard those at risk. Understandably, minority groups seek to extend such regulations to offset more and more of the disadvantages they suffer.

AT WHAT POINT DO WE REGULATE?

Regulations occur whenever people join together to attain a common purpose - from the rules which govern a football match to the requirements of the treaties which establish the World Trade Organisation (WTO). Since smaller communities form part of larger national or international organisations there has to be a choice about the level at which we regulate.

In principle, it might be argued that regulation should occur at the lowest level at which it is likely to be effective. Such an approach allows for the diversity of circumstance and values which is characteristic of the many communities to which we belong. Regulations are more likely to command consent and to be observed without considerable expenditure on enforcement. In practice, people, capital and goods move between communities, so that differences in regulatory regimes may have important implications for the ability of any one group to compete. In such a situation we look to larger groupings in search of what is often described as a 'level playing field'.

The globalisation of the world economy has clear implications for regulation relating to the food industries. If there is to be a level playing field, then the regulatory regime has to cover the whole of the market and to be enforced to uniform standards. Difficulties occur where either of these criteria are breached. The successful conclusion of the Uruguay Round of negotiations in GATT (General Agreement on Tariffs and Trade) represented a modest but significant step forward towards a more open international market in agriculture and foodstuffs. However, as recent disputes between the United States and the European Union (EU) relating to the use of hormones in beef production and the current debate about the acceptability of genetically-modified soya demonstrate, differences in approach to regulation may effectively close markets and negate the expected effects of past agreements. In this situation much will depend upon the acceptance by all parties of the outcome of the WTO disputes settlement procedure.

This demonstrates a second principle influencing the appropriate level at which to regulate. It must correspond to political boundaries within which laws can be enforced. Experience within the EU illustrates both the potential and the difficulties. In the United Kingdom (UK) there is a strong lobby opposed to the transport of live animals for slaughter abroad. This is based partly on the belief that suffering is caused during transport, and partly because the conditions under which animals are maintained and slaughtered in some foreign countries fall far short of those which are acceptable in the UK. A ban on exports would conflict with undertakings relating to trade. The only legitimate way to meet the concerns of the welfare lobbyists would be to apply satisfactory standards of husbandry and transport throughout the EU. A successful move in this direction would clearly constitute a much larger benefit in terms of the welfare of animals than simple bans on the export of live animals for slaughter from one country.

One difficulty is that not all member countries have the same perception of the need to improve matters. Tighter regulations are likely to involve higher costs. Farmers may well argue that they should be compensated, a move likely to be resisted by ministers of finance. The familiar outcome is protracted debate and long time lags in introducing those improvements which are agreed. Whilst it might quite legitimately be argued that the task of British welfare lobbyists should be to change opinion in other countries rather than to demand that the UK government bans trade, action at the domestic level seems more likely to be effective in the short run.

A second difficulty relates to enforcement. Within the EU substantial progress has been made towards harmonising rules relating to welfare but critics remain dissatisfied. As reported in Spedding (1996):

'Increasingly, Governments' actions are harmonised throughout the EU member countries but there are concerns about the extent to which agreements, directives and regulations are implemented, monitored and enforced in different countries. A powerful European Inspectorate must be the ultimate answer to this kind of problem but, whilst discrepancies occur, there is resistance to controls being applied in one country, putting its livestock producers at a competitive disadvantage with those of countries not following the rules. In fact this concern, that advances in animal welfare may impose costs not borne by competitors - whether within the EU or from outside it - is one of the major constraints on progress in this area.'

Whilst the case for international regulation is clear, in practice most regulation which affects the food industries in Europe will continue to be made and enforced by the EU and the nation state. This points out the existence of regulatory frontiers which affect not only the flow of trade but the location of research and investment. In a globalised market, such possibilities represent a real constraint on the ability of national governments or even the EU to regulate.

THE MECHANISMS OF REGULATION - WHO REGULATES WHOM AND HOW?

Politics, policies and information

Regulations are a political activity. As such they have to be implemented *via* the political and legal institutions of each country. Most of these have been shaped by past history. They form part of that network of communication and influence which we call 'the establishment'. It is understandable that those outside this framework should be critical of its operation and demand changes. However, given the changing challenges of regulating a modern food industry, it is always necessary to review the adequacy of existing institutional structures. Within the UK this debate has been given a sharp edge by suggestions that responsibility for food safety should be taken away from the Ministry of Agriculture, Fisheries and Food (MAFF). The proposed appointment of an independent food safety adviser and a committee of advisers to support him, indicates that the government recognises, at least in part, the force of this case.[1]

This Conference provides the key sectors of the industry with opportunities to ventilate their problems and describe their experience. Rightly, if somewhat unconventionally, we have put the consumers at the head of the agenda. We do so because whatever regulatory mechanisms are devised and however they are administered, the ultimate test has to be that they merit and receive the confidence of the consumer. If that is absent, everyone else in the industry will suffer.

A first step in making a regulation has to be to define its target. New targets and priorities emerge *via* the political process. This includes debates within parties, campaigns by pressure groups or the media and complaints about the working of present arrangements from those most immediately affected within industry. Many claim to speak for 'consumers'. The National Consumer Council (NCC) is specifically funded by the Department of Trade and Industry to represent the interests of consumers. It has taken a continuing interest in food policy (see, for example, NCC, 1988). Those who make regulations have to judge the claims made by such organisations and balance them with other competing interests.

Successful regulation demands much more than a generally good intention. There is a need for information, for an understanding of how the industry operates and how it might respond to various types of regulatory device. There must also be an analysis of what costs and benefits might be involved and upon whom they would fall. Existing information cannot be assumed to provide an adequate picture of the industry for regulations which involve new areas. Those who seek new regulations or want to change existing systems usually present their own data. However, this may be partial, inaccurate or irrelevant. This has to be sifted and tested. In the process governments need to consult with those who have special knowledge of the issues involved. This must include the food industry itself, but it will also involve pressure groups and private individuals who have researched the area concerned. In the food industry the need for consultation is so frequent that government has established committees, such as the Food Advisory Committee, for the purpose. It needs to be an open and public process so that there is a genuine opportunity for non-establishment voices to be heard. Where there are important gaps in information there may need to be specific enquiries. This can be a long drawn out process but if it is unduly hurried the result is likely to be bad regulation.

Policy makers' links with industry and others

Effective regulation within the food industry requires an understanding of the way in which it operates. Without this, regulations which may appear commonsense to the outsider may be ineffective or destructive. Governments, even though they may seek to operate at arm's length and apply the general principles of a 'free market' need much detailed understanding of the functioning of an industry which is to be regulated. Specialist ministries, such as MAFF, are in constant communication with their sector and may be expected to have a good appreciation of how it might respond. This implies a sustained dialogue with the industry, its representatives and sometimes individual businesses. Where existing links with the industry are weak, then a substantial effort will be needed to ensure that a balanced picture of how it operates is obtained.

A particular problem arises in the food industry, where the same regulation may apply to firms of very different size. For a major multi-national equipped with specialist legal and accountancy staff it may cause few difficulties. For the small family firm where the proprietor has very largely to be his own accountant, technologist and legal advisor it may require hiring costly external expertise and/or diverting management effort from productive activity. To apply less stringent rules to small companies may lead to distortion and run the risk that unsafe product reaches a market. It will also create threshold problems which discourage the growth of successful small enterprises.

In the course of their dialogue with government, industries will naturally present their information and analysis in ways which seem likely to make any new regulation as advantageous as possible. This raises anxieties that the Ministry concerned may be captured by its industry. To put this input into perspective it is thus necessary for the regulator to consult a wider range of opinion. One obvious source of input are the pressure groups which have campaigned for a regulation. Whilst the direction of their advice will be clear and its quality may vary, many established groups have genuine expertise which may include matters beyond the horizon of the industry itself. Voluntary groups often claim the right to be heard because they represent sections of the community which might otherwise be neglected. Pressure groups themselves gain legitimacy from being seen to be consulted. Even if their views are not accepted, their involvement reassures their supporters of their influence and effectiveness. Public disagreement may even enhance their image by making it clear that they have not been captured by the establishment.

Whilst input from pressure groups and overt consultations must be a fully public activity, some of the material which government needs in order to devise regulations is likely to be commercially sensitive. Companies who provide it need to know it will not be passed on to competitors. In the absence of such information regulations may be designed for yesterday's industry rather than that in which they are to apply. This results in inevitable tensions between the need to protect commercial confidence, the wish to pursue processes of open government and the importance of being seen to act without undue influence from the industry.

Governments and commentators tend to unite around the notion that regulations must be based on 'sound science' (see Fisk, 1996) and consultation with research workers who have explored relevant areas can be of great value in shaping regulations. However, the issues are far from simple. At least two sorts of problem arise. Science at any one point of time is always provisional. It offers no certainties, only the most complete account of the chain of cause and effect as it is currently understood. The function of research is to replace this account by another. Inevitably there is a politically uncomfortable moment at which the advice provided by 'sound scientists' changes. A second problem is that scientists seldom speak with unanimity. Any government has to choose which version at any one time it is to regard as 'sound'. Processes of peer review, repetition of experiments etc provide an establishment view but they still cannot escape the discomfort which arises when the heretic proves to be right. The range of views amongst which governments have to decide is substantial. They include differing views about what consumers want (see, for example, *Food irradiation - the consumers' view* (1990) by the Consumer Association) and varying evaluations of the scientific evidence, (for example, Snell (1986)).

Implementation
The regulators, having clarified what the intended target is, have to consider how best it might be implemented. The cost to both industry and the administration has to be assessed and related to the effectiveness of the regime instituted. Where regulations have to apply across several countries and through varying political and bureaucratic

25

mechanisms, there is a need to consider not just what is 'sound science' but the ways in which regulations based on it will be applied and interpreted in all the countries concerned. Where, as with EU Directives, the application is left to an important degree to national governments, then the regulators concerned will be under pressure to ensure that the way in which the rules operate does not unduly penalise their own citizens.

The UK approach to both politics and law tends to be confrontational rather than consensual. At the regulatory level this translates into prescriptive rather than indicative rules for industry. Such arrangements make it possible to identify defaulters and to prosecute successfully those who have failed, but there is a danger of introducing undue rigidity. Detailed specification enables prosecutions to be undertaken on the basis that the regulation has been broken even if the purpose which it is intended to serve has been achieved. To shield both the civil servant and the minister from the risk that a loophole may be revealed which defeats the purpose of the regulation, there is a natural tendency to attempt to cover all possible circumstances. The result may be lengthy, complex sets of rules which require specialist expertise to interpret and apply.

For many food regulations the goals of the policy are shared by all parties - eg to ensure that food is safe. However, if this becomes translated into over-precise rules, it may result in costs without any substantial increase in effectiveness. By making regulations that operate in a more indicative manner, setting targets but leaving the businesses concerned more scope to determine the means by which they are attained can be both more effective and less costly. However, such an approach is not without its problems. Government has to strike an acceptable balance between allowing enforcement agencies and businesses sensible discretion in the application of regulations, and the risk of corruption. Those countries which get this right are likely to enjoy both more effective regulation and a competitive advantage.

Regulation and responsibility
Whatever the mechanism used to formulate and enforce regulations, the ultimate responsibility has to be that of the Government as a whole. It is dangerous and probably untrue to say that MAFF operates on behalf of the agricultural and food industries, if by that it is implied it does not operate in the national interest. Quite rightly it has to present clearly the impact of regulations on the industries with which it is concerned, but decisions about how to respond must be for the government as a whole.

To be successful, regulatory mechanisms have to command the confidence of those to whom they are applied and on whose behalf they were written. The merits of the case for establishing some food agency separate from MAFF may owe more to perception than to solving the really difficult problems governments face in regulating the food industry. However, from the perspective of the industry, if such an agency does reassure the public it may well be worthwhile. However, food scares will still arise, governments will still have to take the ultimate decisions based on evidence which is always incomplete, and lobbyists will make it their mission to inform and influence a new agency just as they do the MAFF.

THE REALITY OF RISK

It may please lawyers seeking damages and comfort those who believe life should be free from stress to assume that governments should know everything and legislate to avoid all unpleasant outcomes. However, such an approach bears no relationship to the practical limitations of what may be achieved by regulation. Not only does 'sound science' fail to provide certainty, regulators have to operate in an area of economic, political and natural risks. Even where the balance of scientific evidence points to one approach, other considerations and risks may suggest a quite different course of action.

The California law commonly referred to as 'Proposition 65' illustrates the sort of difficult political balancing act which may be involved. This requires warning labels to be placed on all products which contain chemicals which can cause cancer or birth defects. Amongst these is vitamin A which, according to the State of California, may cause birth defects. However, simultaneously the federal government is pushing vitamin A as a key ingredient in its push for improved nutrition (McKinney, 1994). Regulators have to choose whether the dangers are likely to exceed the benefits and to frame regulations which convey the information in forms which enable consumers to make informed choices. The assumption that governments should or even can provide precise guidance to consumers about such issues is unrealistic.

Even where a risk is identified and its likely incidence can be quantified, there has to be a careful examination of whether regulations are the most cost-effective way of dealing with it. In some cases, better public information may be both cheaper and more effective. In others, for example, where there is a statistical risk of 1:1 000 000 that a pesticide residue will cause cancer, governments have to take account of the costs of banning the substance in relation to the benefits it brings. In such situations it may be politically difficult to admit, but the national interest may best be served by doing nothing about the pesticide and investing in improved methods for the early detection and effective treatment of cancer.

WHEN, HOW AND WHY DO WE DEREGULATE?

One of the paradoxes of much current debate is that, at a time when there are claims for more and more effective regulations relating to food, there exists a widespread belief that our economy suffers from too many and too detailed regulations. Thus the Government has established a 'Deregulation Task Force' with a view to lifting the burden of excessive regulation from industry. Its publication, *Good regulatory principles and practice in Europe*, includes a 'Deregulation Checklist for Ministers'. It is then worthwhile to note at this stage some of the reasons for deregulation.

Obsolescence

The balance of cost effectiveness in regulation is continually changing as market patterns shift and scientific understanding grows. Thus, an unchanging set of regulations may impose growing rigidity on the food industry and consumers without enhancing food safety or enabling consumers to make more informed judgements. Particular problems arise where the introduction of new forms of food processing can be impeded because manufacturers or retailers are constrained by regulations designed to ensure that traditionally prepared foods would be safe. Minimally, the risk of obsolescence requires continued monitoring of regulations and the way in which they are enforced. Periodically, whole areas of regulation may safely be scrapped since the practices to which they relate are no longer used.

Redundancy

Legislation dealing with differing issues may impact on the same industrial process - for example, requirements relating to working time and legal restraints on the employment of young people. Later legislation may cover much the same ground, but by slight variations in wording or method of administration, result in confusion for those who are supposed to apply it. Revising existing regulations to take account of later law may make it possible to dispose of some redundant arrangements.

A particular source of redundancy arises where European law covers much the same ground as national law. In such a situation the EU law has primacy and the existence of unchanged national regulations, which more or less duplicate its provisions, may mislead. The revision and scrapping of redundant legislation avoids costly litigation.

Complexity

Regulations may become more complex either because the external world changes in a way not foreseen by their authors or because of the incremental process of updating.[2] Changes in other regulations, for example those relating to equal opportunities, may require revision of regulations designed in earlier decades. Updating, to take account of rulings by the European Court, which may be drafted in a different language and on the basis of different legal traditions, can result in complications as existing regulations are adjusted.

Complexity on this scale can lead to a situation in which the requirement of the law becomes unclear. Legal advice and guidance from civil servant administrators may vary. In such a situation the outcome of the regulation becomes arbitrary, oppressive for the industry and uncertain in its effect. Its removal or replacement becomes essential.

Enforcement failures

Enforcement may fail either in the obvious sense that the regulation is not observed or, less obviously, because its enforcement proves to have unforeseen and disproportionate burdens on those to whom it applies.

If the cost of enforcement exceeds the amount which the authorities are prepared to invest in the process, it is likely that a regulation will be at best partially effective. If an enforcement system suffers from corruption, then it may be applied in ways which line the pockets of enforcers rather than protect the public. If a regulation is designed in such a way that evidence of compliance cannot be readily and reasonably provided it is unlikely to be applied as intended.

Regulations that impose excessive burdens on industry may prevent the evil they are intended to combat by effectively extinguishing the industry itself. Firms that wish to survive simply relocate to less restrictive regulatory environments or cease to trade in the area affected. Where this means lost employment or the demise of most small businesses in the sector, the effect of the regulation may well be judged to have gone well beyond the intended target.

Failures of competition

Regulations that impose costs on businesses may also become an instrument of protection. By insisting that all operators invest in some costly piece of equipment, companies who have already equipped themselves and large organisations who can readily afford to do so, may deter newcomers and force small businesses out. Businesses may also argue that the same rules should be applied to producers in other countries or imports should be banned. It seems unfair to allow foreign enterprises to compete in domestic markets using techniques that are illegal for home producers, but such regulations can prove effective non-tariff barriers, shielding high-cost domestic suppliers from competition.

Within the international community and on an even more regular basis within the EU, a great deal of attention is focused on the ways in which regulations impact on particular countries. Since the 'devil is generally in the detail', effective international regulation requires close understanding by civil servants of the implications of alternative wordings for the industries within their own countries. If the impact of an agreed regulation, as it is applied, is regarded as unacceptable, then countries which suffer are likely to seek its repeal or modification. Current tensions within the EU's milk regime provide a contemporary example.

THE REGULATORS AND THE PUBLIC

The substance of this paper and of others which will follow is that regulation of the food and agricultural industries is complex and the need for and effects of regulation are ever changing. One result of this is that from time to time failures occur. For some individuals those failures may be catastrophic. As a result, the dangers that lurk within the food chain must always be taken seriously. However, one response to recent food scares has been to condemn the regulator. This is itself dangerous if it leads ordinary people to turn away from the best available science and resort to the nostrums of quacks and food fanatics.

There is thus a need for considered dispassionate analysis of ways in which the institutional structure of food regulation might be improved. The fervour with which some groups seize upon every failure or rumour of failure to dangle an unwary public over the pit of food disaster owes more to the techniques of fundamentalist preachers than to the patient search for understanding upon which we all depend. Such outbursts may say more about the political ambition of their authors than about food safety.

Among the propagandist phrases that commonly flow over this debate are two which add more to confusion than to enlightenment, 'sound science' and 'independent regulators'. Sufficient has been said about the nature of science to make it clear that it cannot remove risk from decisions and that, as understanding grows, it will from time to time require changes in existing regulations. It is also clear that without adequate input from the industries they regulate, regulatory authorities can easily inflict avoidable damage on those who work in food and agriculture without any significant gain to the rest of society. If 'independence' is taken to mean that the food industry has no influence over the way it is regulated, the outcome may well represent the triumph of ignorance. The duty of regulatory authorities has to be to balance one set of claims against others. To do that they must be in a position to test claims from any source - including claims of those who assert that they 'represent the consumer'.

Quite rightly, the composition of regulatory authorities needed to achieve balance will change. It is healthy that such a debate should occur. Ultimately, however the authority is constituted, if propagandists exploit each food scare to discredit the regulator's credentials, public confidence will be lost. Perhaps we need not just a new food safety agency or a food safety supremo, but a new sense of responsibility and maturity among those who write and comment on this vital industry.

REFERENCES

Consumer Association (1990) *Food irradiation - the consumers' view*. London: Survey Research Group, The Association for Consumers' Research.

Deregulation Unit, Cabinet Office (1995) *Deregulation Task Force Report 1994/1995*. London: HMSO.

Deregulation Unit, Cabinet Office (1997) *Good regulatory principles and practice in Europe*. London: The Stationery Office.

Fisk, D (1996) *Sound science and UK environmental policy*. Paper given to the London Diplomatic Science Club, May 1996. [Unpublished]

Food, Drink and Agriculture Task Force (1994) *Proposals for deregulation*. Deposited in the House of Commons Library. [Unpublished]

McKinney, L C (1994) Workable food safety regulation. *Choices* (Second Quarter), 10-14.

McKinney, L C (1994) Setting workable regulatory thresholds. In: *Food and agricultural markets: the food revolution*. Washington DC: National Planning Association.

National Consumer Council (1988) *Food policy and the consumer*. London: National Consumer Council.

Snell, P (1986) *Pesticide residues in food - the case for real control*. London: The London Food Commission.

Spedding, C R W (1996) *Agriculture and the citizen*. London: Chapman and Hall.

NOTES

1 The appointment of an 'independent food safety adviser' and a supporting committee of advisers, was announced by the Minister of Agriculture, Fisheries and Food on 30 January 1997. The aim was to restore confidence in British products.

2 An example of the first process is the development of fish farming - is this to be classified as part of agriculture, in which case legislation

relating to minimum wages for that industry apply, or as part of the fishing industry which is not subject to these rules. The Agricultural Wages order attempts to help:- "AGRICULTURE" has the meaning assigned to it in section 17 of the Act [the Agricultural Wages Act 1948] (that is 'agriculture' includes dairy-farming, the production of any consumable produce which is grown for sale or for consumption or other use for the purposes of trade or business or of any other undertaking (whether carried on for profit or not), and the use of land as grazing, meadow or pasture land or orchard or osier land or woodland or for market gardens or nursery grounds).

DISCUSSION

Ms Annabel Holt (Annabel's Crusade for the Environment) referred to the issues of safety and risk, which she said are odd bed-fellows; she believed the main need is to look at how to regulate safety as, at the moment, the allowable risks are too great. She urged that everybody present should consider the matter of safety tests for humans using tissue cultures, as to use animals to test for human safety is unscientific methodology.

Professor Marsh, in reply, said that the full version of his paper to be published in the proceedings, includes paragraphs on the scientific aspects. He agreed that we do have a problem in terms of both the authorities upon which we rely, and upon the developments which take place within those authorities. Science itself is a process of scepticism, of formulating hypotheses and of dismissing them. It is a process that takes place against a background of increasing capacity in terms of technology and therefore, we do need to be looking at new, appropriate and effective means of coping with the challenges presented *via* food safety and indeed many other issues in our society.

Marshall BJ & Miller FA (Eds)(1997) *Management of regulation in the food chain - balancing costs, benefits and effects.*
CAS Paper 36. Reading: Centre for Agricultural Strategy.

2 Food regulation - the consumer agenda

Sheila McKechnie

INTRODUCTION

The past year has seen consumer confidence in the management of our food supply reach an all-time low. Consumers have little confidence that the government has their interests at heart when regulating food. This clearly needs to be addressed - the food chain is becoming increasingly complex and dominated by advances in food technology.

Food safety is still a major problem in this country. Reported cases of food poisoning continue to rise. But not only is the number of people becoming infected on the increase, the severity of these infections is also becoming much more serious. Cases of *Salmonella enteritidis* may not be increasing as rapidly as they did at the end of the 1980s, but the second most common cause of *Salmonella* food poisoning (*S. typhimurium* DT104) is now resistant to six commonly used antibiotics. We have also recently seen how *Salmonella* can survive in foods once considered low risk - as the recent withdrawal of Milumil powdered baby milk demonstrates. And of more immediate concern we have the threat of VTEC (Verocytotoxin)-producing strains of *Escherichia coli* (eg 0157) which is a particular threat to the young and the elderly as Scotland has unfortunately had to discover: 0157 may be our main concern today, but other serotypes have already caused outbreaks in other countries.

Other diet-related diseases continue to be a problem. In *The health of the nation* (1992), the government made a commitment to tackle the major causes of death in this country: coronary heart disease and cancer. Nutrition is an important part of this, but the Nutrition Task Force was disbanded after only three years. And of course we are still waiting to find out the true public health impact of the mismanagement

33

of the Bovine Spongiform Encephalopathy (BSE) crisis. The longer it takes before we hear of the next victim of new-variant Creutzfeldt-Jacob Disease (CJD) the more secure we can feel. But should consumers really be playing this waiting game?

FUTURE PROBLEMS AND PROSPECTS
The future looks even more complicated. We need to be certain that there are adequate controls in place to protect public health. Genetic modification is already having a major impact on our food supply - although most of us don't know about it. Scientists cannot even agree on the nature of the risk when it comes to assessing these foods - as the European Scientific Committee on Foods (SCF) decision about the unprocessed Ciba-Geigy maize shows; it decided the risk was acceptable - the Advisory Committee on Novel Foods and Processes (ACNFP) thought it was not.

Alongside this we have had a deregulation initiative that has removed many compositional standards. We welcome increased consumer choice - but consumers need to know what this choice is and have adequate information to make an informed choice about the content of foods they buy. Unfortunately, labelling information has not always been so forthcoming. A survey carried out by the Consumers' Association (CA) last year showed that consumers felt that the government gave priority to producer and political interests. Two thirds believed that the influence food producers have results in a policy that is against the interests of consumers. More than half of the people we interviewed thought that government departments were least trustworthy for impartial advice on food safety.

PRINCIPLES OF FOOD REGULATION
This brings me to the fundamental consumer principles which should be an integral part of any food regulation system, but which have sadly been undermined in recent years:

Access
For some of us, there has never been access to a greater range of foods. Unfortunately, this is not the case for all consumers. Low-income consumers should have access to affordable food and the difficulties of achieving a healthier diet need to be recognised.

Choice
Consumers should be able to choose a healthy and safe diet and have the option to avoid foods that they do not wish to eat. Genetically-modified foods are a good example of this. The nature of this

technology means that some consumers may wish to avoid them for ethical reasons. They may also wish to avoid them because they are concerned about the long-term environmental or health effects. This is why we have always said that foods produced using genetic modification should be labelled. In the case of the soya, it is an issue of consumer choice rather than safety. The unfortunate decision by soya producers in the USA to mix genetically-modified soya in with standard soya has denied consumers this right.

Information
Informative labelling is an important aspect of choice. As choice increases and consumers become more aware of the importance of healthy eating, their demand for easy-to-understand and accurate information about the foodstuffs on offer increases. Food claims about nutritional content and health benefits need to be more tightly regulated to give consumers effective protection against misleading claims. We need information about how to prepare and cook foods safely - warnings should be put on high-risk foods and food safety advice needs to be regularly reiterated. Consumers increasingly need information about the complex methods used to produce food. We want to know about all ingredients, for example, if water has been added to food, or if mechanically-recovered meat or offal are used. We should also know whether or not it contains any irradiated ingredients or is genetically modified. But as well as labelling, consumers need to have sufficient information to enable them to understand what the concerns are and what these processes and ingredients are, so that they can weigh up the potential risks and benefits for themselves.

Safety
Consumers expect that if food is on sale it is safe. But it is not that simple. The Food Safety Act 1990 states that food should not be injurious to health, but the problem is that in a lot of cases the dangers associated with foods will not be seen in the short term. The development of resistant strains of bacteria and the constantly shrinking range of effective antibiotics is one example. BSE has shown how a simple change in a process that was thought fairly insignificant at the time can have devastating consequences. This is why we need to develop clear ways of assessing risks where there is an absence of conclusive scientific evidence. This should not be interpreted to mean that if there is no scientific information available to say that it is unsafe, it can be assumed that it is safe. Decisions must always be based on the precautionary principle and public health considerations must come first, not just eagerness to get a product on the market in order to compete with foreign industries. We have seen what happens when the interests of industry come first over public health - they lose out in the long-run as much as consumers do.

It must also be ensured that there is greater openness about who funds research and that there is a coordinated approach to research so that work in the public interest is funded. We also believe that research should be subject to peer review so that suitable 'weighting' is given to research in order that unsound and inconclusive science is not given unnecessary significance - and we know when a piece of research can be interpreted as 'the gold standard' by which food safety decisions can be made.

Redress
If we have a problem with a food - if it makes us ill or if we are misled about the nature of the food - there should be a suitable course of action. There are provisions in the Food Safety Act that provide for this, but it is not so clear cut with some foods. What about BSE? After all we were categorically told that beef and beef products were safe to eat. The CA has recently carried out a lot of work looking at dietary supplements - an area where there is a lot of confusion about who has responsibility for dealing with problems - should we look to the Ministry of Agriculture, Fisheries and Food (MAFF), the Department of Health, The Medicines Control Agency or the local Trading Standards Officer?

Quality
Food quality has been open to many different interpretations. Many consumers will not want, or be able to pay premium prices for, premium-quality food. They expect to have a choice. The trouble is that new processes have meant that food can be produced more cheaply, but this is not always made obvious to consumers. Concerns about genetically-modified soya also demonstrate people's lack of awareness of the widespread use of soya in processed foods - many of us assumed we hardly ever ate soya. Consumers should be able to expect a certain quality - or know that they are choosing to buy a cheaper product. Quality standards have been undermined, but consumers have not always been informed of the changes.

Value for money
Without information about the content of food, consumers cannot assess value for money. This information needs to be straightforward and consistent. For example, the development of Quantitative Ingredient Declarations - showing the percentages of the main ingredients present - will be an important way for consumers to judge.

NEED TO ADDRESS AND RESOLVE MYTHS AND UNCERTAINTIES

Perhaps the reason for the failure to acknowledge these key consumer principles stems from the following three myths that have emerged in recent years:

'A co-ordinated, pro-active food policy is 'nannying''

Giving people adequate information to ensure that they know how to choose a healthy diet and are not misled by products that are on sale is not 'nannying'. If we are to see a decline in the incidence of food poisoning, or we are to achieve nutritional and dietary targets there needs to be a coordinated approach to food policy. That is, setting clear criteria that will ensure that the fundamental consumer principles are taken into account when regulating the food chain - and making sure that all departments and ministries with responsibility for food have a consistent approach and work towards the same goals.

'Consumers are mad and react irrationally to food scares'

This stems from a comment made by the Secretary of State for Health during the BSE crisis. Apparently, it was not the cows that were mad; it was consumers. I do not think that consumers reacted irrationally to the BSE crisis. In fact I am surprised that the statistics suggest that the market has recovered so soon. Consumer concerns over the failure to regulate adequately and the remaining uncertainties about BSE should not be dismissed as irrational. Despite what United Kingdom (UK) officials appear to have told the Committee of Inquiry set up by the European Parliament, BSE was not an 'act of God', it could have been prevented. This attitude demonstrates clearly the need for a culture change, not just structure, if we are to see consumers' concerns addressed.

'Regulation is unnecessary, bureaucratic and prevents innovation'

Innovation is all well and good, but if it progresses unchecked one runs the risk of losing consumer confidence which in the long run will be devastating for business. Regulation does not prevent innovation; it ensures that public health and consumer concerns are not forgotten along the way. It is essential that a cost/benefit analysis for consumers is carried out as well as a cost/compliance assessment for industry.

We have recently seen what happens if we go too far down the deregulation route. It is highly likely that the BSE epidemic in cattle was the result of deregulation. The interim report of The Pennington Group (1997) on *E. coli* has called for greater and more specific regulation reversing, to some extent, the move away from prescriptive food safety legislation. We are in favour of a 'hazard analysis' approach, but there also has to be an acknowledgement that this is not going to be easily implemented at all stages of the food chain. This is why we think there should be licensing of all food premises before they open so that it can be ensured they reach an appropriate standard before consumers are put at risk. It is also vital that enforcement officers have the powers to act immediately when there is a risk to public health.

These three myths have I believe led to five specific failings of the current system:

- We have lost the primacy of public health; we constantly witness a bizarre situation where measures to protect public health are balanced against their impact on industry.
- The ministry responsible for protecting consumer interests also has dual responsibility for promoting the interests of industry; the way that BSE has been handled demonstrates clearly how untenable this position is. We now appear to be facing a similar conflict of interest with genetically-modified foods; consumer concerns have not been fully addressed.
- There is a lack of transparency in the decision-making process - the public does not have access to the information upon which government decisions are based; despite several requests we have not been able to see the information that has been considered by the Spongiform Encephalopathies Advisory Committee (SEAC).
- There is a failure to acknowledge scientific uncertainty and the need for a multi-disciplinary approach; this was clearly amiss throughout the BSE crisis, both at European Union and UK levels. SEAC did not have a public health representative until December 1995. But the lessons have not been learned (as the approval of unprocessed maize demonstrates).
- There is a lack of effective consumer involvement and representation, the most obvious example being the failure to appoint a consumer representative to SEAC. Consumer representation should not be viewed as tokenistic - we have a valuable part to play. We can ensure that the right questions are posed and that the workings of these committees are open to public scrutiny.

CONCLUSIONS

Food policy is clearly on the agenda for the next election with the proposals for a Food Safety Council and a Food Standards Agency. We will shortly be publishing our model for restructuring of the current system. We support any proposal that addresses similar concerns about food control in Europe. But the government's plans for a Food Safety Council do not, I believe, tackle the problems I have outlined. We do not need a tepid attempt to restore 'consumer confidence' without acknowledging the fundamental problems within the,current framework. We, therefore, still firmly believe that the only way that consumers' concerns will be addressed in the long term, is by the establishment of an independent national food agency.

REFERENCES

Department of Health (1992) *The health of the nation: a strategy for health in England.* London: HMSO

The Pennington Group (1997) *Report on the circumstances leading to the 1996 outbreak of infection with E. coli 0157 in Central Scotland. The implications for food safety and the lessons to be learned.* London: The Stationery Office.

DISCUSSION

Mrs Joanna Wheatley (Farmer) wished to follow up two points. Firstly, that there is a tremendous problem if a chemical is causing ill-health or poisoning because of the difficulty over burden of proof and in actually isolating the particular chemical which is causing the problem. And secondly, in relation to the BSE débâcle, where in her view the scientists involved have not looked fully at the possibility that we may not be faced with a cross from species to species, but that we may actually be looking at a common trigger that may be a toxin. True science would look at all the culprits and use a process of elimination, which she considered had not actually been done in this case; the problem as she saw it, is one of burden of proof and untangling, in a world where we now use so many different toxic substances.

Ms Sheila McKechnie, in reply, said that if you wait until you actually know what the agent is - and those who understand public health or epidemiology will recognise the 'Broad Street Pump' analogy - major changes to protect public health have not been based on detailed scientific knowledge, but on epidemiological knowledge. She felt that there is a great difference between epidemiologists and clinicians, and urged that the former should be more involved in food regulation. On the question of the processes of proof, she commented that in civil cases the balance of proof is not 'beyond all reasonable doubt' but is based on a 'balance of probabilities'.

Marshall BJ & Miller FA (Eds)(1997) *Management of regulation in the food chain - balancing costs, benefits and effects.*
CAS Paper 36. Reading: Centre for Agricultural Strategy.

3 Food regulation and the retail sector

Nigel Matthews

THE CONSUMER INTEREST

May I first of all say that I find it quite unusual to appear at a Conference quite so high up in the batting order. I have spoken on a number of occasions at conferences on food regulation and retailing and I have found that invariably the batting order starts with a representative from the producers; then there is somebody from the manufacturing side; then there may be somebody from Government or the public authorities; then there is a retailer and, finally, there is someone representing the consumer. I congratulate today's organisers for breaking with tradition and starting with the consumer. This is an important innovation because, in the area of food regulation, the consumer interest has not always been given the weight it requires.

Whatever may have been the background to a particular piece of legislation in the past - protection of the farming community, the politics of the Common Agricultural Policy (CAP) or the removal of non-tariff barriers, nowadays legislation needs to concentrate on the consumer. Adopting this perspective will involve substantial changes to the CAP regime. That does not mean that all suggestions and proposals by consumer organisations or interest groups for regulatory intervention should be accepted. We need to bear in mind that regulations that impose unnecessary change, reduce flexibility, or provide undue protection to one sector or another, will impose additional costs on the food chain, which will be passed on to the customer. Consideration of new regulation and candidates for deregulation must be based on a proper analysis of the problem and against accepted criteria.

THE PLACE OF THE RETAILER

It is right that the retailer should come second in the batting order after the consumer because he directly interfaces with the consumer, transmitting consumer requirements back to the ultimate producer. Food retailing, at whatever level, is a highly competitive business. The range of choice, the availability of outlets and product alternatives exist as never before. Food retailers of whatever size or format only succeed by satisfying the customer not once, but day-in day-out throughout the year. It is this more than any amount of regulation that drives our businesses and is the touchstone of our success. The retailer exists not as the handmaid of the manufacturer or the producer but as the interpreter of the consumers' demands in the market place. Increasingly, it is the retailer who has the information to make the decision about what it is the customer wants and what he must seek to supply. As a result, the food chain is increasingly becoming a partnership, disciplined by competition and led by the retailer as the interpreter of the customers' wishes. Competition is a real discipline. It goes beyond questions of mere price. In satisfying the consumer, the retailer must ensure that the unwritten contract of trust which exists between the two is honoured.

In the food chain, regulations come in a variety of shapes and sizes. They do not all have the same purpose. There are regulations and laws that apply to food safety; other regulations are concerned with providing consumer information; others with product composition, single market regulations to prevent distortion of trade, and produce marketing regulations designed to support the CAP. Then again, there are regulations on many other matters which affect the food retailer as a retailer which are not specifically about food.

FOOD SAFETY

As far as food safety is concerned, it may be trite, but I think it is important to stress that retailers have an overriding concern to supply safe, wholesome food to their customers. We are less concerned with the **enforcement of regulations** than with the **application of good practices** designed to lead to safe food handling and to assure safe food. This is an intensely practical matter and it colours our view of regulation and the way legislation ought to be developed. It is also an important matter of attitude and if I may I would like to digress and show you how it is applied within Sainsbury's.

The Sainsbury's supermarket business comprises 370 supermarket stores, 21 000 different product lines, and 110 000 staff, serving 8.5 million customers every week. More than half of Sainsbury's products are sold under our own name. We work closely with our suppliers and apply formal detailed methods of hazard analysis under the Hazard

Analysis Critical Control Points (HACCP) procedure which is internationally recognised as the most effective way of maximising product safety. We regard it as an essential component in designing processes and assuring product safety. Under the Sainsbury's Product Management System, it is a fundamental requirement that all suppliers adopt the HACCP approach to managing the safety and quality of their products. We carry this risk analysis approach through into our stores where it underpins our staff-training programmes and procedures.

Another example of our concerns for food safety is the development of our farm-assured meat programme. This started in 1990 with a pioneering scheme, and now covers 9000 selected livestock farms. Each farm is rigorously inspected, and all steers are fed a grass-based diet. Regular meetings are held between producers, processors and our own management and all fresh meat on display in stores is clearly labelled 'Farm Assured'.

I could give you many other examples from my own Company on how we seek in practice to achieve the objectives set out in the Food Safety Act.

REGULATION AND DEREGULATION
This leads me to a particularly important point, namely that the lack of a specific regulation on an issue does not mean that there is no legislative requirement on the retailer or indeed on anybody else in the food chain. The Food Safety Act itself is a major umbrella which lays down an overall objective with which we must comply. It is a good and comprehensive framework that can be complemented by Codes of Practice which themselves set out best practice in the industry as it develops. Focusing on the requirements of the Food Safety Act and the use of industry codes of best practice offer the opportunity to consolidate and simplify many existing regulations. Specific regulation may be necessary and helpful for some matters. But regulation on its own does not achieve the objective of safe food; what matters is to lay down proper procedures based on an analysis and understanding of risk and to apply them day-by-day. It is through the dull routine of applying best practice rather than the dramatic action of new regulation, that safe food is achieved.

Against that background, where do we stand on deregulation? It will be no surprise for you to learn that we fully support the attempts being made by Government to ensure that regulations do not inhibit business unnecessarily and do not impose unnecessary burdens upon it.

HISTORY OF DEREGULATION

The following is a brief review of some of the milestones in recent years:

October 1992
Deregulation initiative relaunched at Conservative Party Conference

Early 1993
The Rt Hon Michael Heseltine, MP asks Lord Sainsbury of Preston Candover, KG to chair the 7 business Task Forces

Late 1993
Task Forces put forward 605 recommendations for deregulatory action

Mid 1994
Deregulation and Contracting Out Act becomes law

New Deregulation Task Force of 20 businessmen set up

Cabinet Office Deregulation Unit tasked with taking forward the crusade under the guidance of The Rt Hon Roger Freeman MP, Chancellor of the Duchy of Lancaster

March 1985
Government's efficiency unit publishes its report *Burdens on business*

June 1985
Government respond to the report with the White Paper *Lifting the burdens*.

DEREGULATION AT THE COMMUNITY LEVEL

There is an echo in the European Union (EU) of the approach that the British Government has adopted. The Sutherland Report (CEC, 1992) in looking at single market regulation, proposed that the principles for good regulation should be:
- need
- effectiveness
- proportionality
- consistency
- communication

Other key steps in the European sector were the 1995 Anglo-German Businessmen's Report *Deregulation Now* and the European Commission's publication of the *Molitor Report* (CEC, 1995) with 109 recommendations for deregulatory action and its 'SLIM' Initiative aimed at simplifying and rationalising legislation.

Sainsbury's has been heavily involved in aspects of this exercise from the beginning. Like many businesses, we responded to Government initiatives providing information on the impact of individual regulations. Lord Sainsbury of Preston Candover, KG, our former Chairman, was at one time special advisor on deregulation to The Rt Hon Michael Heseltine, MP. Even with the full force of the Prime Minister's authority and that of Senior Cabinet Ministers, the Deregulation and Contracting Out Act and the activities of the Deregulation Unit, deregulation has been, and is, an uphill struggle.

When the initiative was relaunched in 1992, I was quoted in the report as saying that my colleagues were 'facing a veritable blizzard of regulations'. That metaphor was apposite but if you will indulge me a little I will offer you a slightly different one this morning, taken from that eulogy to convenience food by Lewis Carroll, *The Walrus and the Carpenter*. You will recall that those two characters went for a walk and took some oysters and ate them.

> The Walrus and the Carpenter
> Were walking close at hand;
> They wept like anything to see
> Such quantities of sand:
> "If this were only cleared away"
> They said, "it *would* be grand!"
>
> "If seven maids with seven mops
> Swept it for half a year
> Do you suppose," the Walrus said,
> "That they could get it clear?"
> "I doubt it," said the Carpenter,
> And shed a bitter tear.

The food industry recognises that the sand will not be swept clean; and that we will not get rid of many of the detailed regulations that have built up over the years. Furthermore, we do not, as I have already said, seek to do away with all laws affecting the food chain. It is essential that there is a proper legal regulation of the food chain, and emphasis on deregulation and change must not be taken as suggesting the contrary. However, what is important now is to ensure that the regulations that we have are appropriate, that they achieve their objectives and that new regulations are not introduced unless they are essential. So whilst the sand will not be swept clean we may avoid a new tide bringing yet more sand up to the beach.

Achieving this objective is difficult since dynamic Government invariably seeks to justify its existence by new laws. It is also complicated by the overlapping consequences of EU activity. The attempt to regulate temperature controls is a prime example (see Figure 1). In the UK we have achieved a sensible compromise but we are a long way from that in the EU.

Figure 1
Temperature requirements under EU vertical hygiene directives

The Fresh Meat (Hygiene and Inspection) Regs 1992	Fresh meat +7°C Offal +3°C
The Poultry Meat Etc. (Hygiene and Inspection) Regs 1994	Poultry +4°C
The Wild Game (Hygiene and Inspection) Regs 1995	Large wild game meat +7°C Small wild game meat +4°C
The Meat Products (Hygiene) Regs 1994	Maximum of +8°C
Minced Meat and Meat Preparations (Hygiene) Regs 1995	+2°C
Dairy Products (Hygiene) Regs 1995	+6°C

This is a matrix of the temperature requirements set by the various vertical directives of the EC. It is fine provided you are dealing in one commodity only but quite impractical when you are dealing, as modern retailers do, across the whole spectrum. Our arguments for a more rational and practical system are making heavy weather. Eventually we have succeeded in achieving a general directive on food hygiene and with it a commitment to review the existing vertical hygiene directive. But this commitment is embroiled in a dispute between the different Directorates-General of the EC over their various competences. This dispute has tended to overshadow arguments for coherence and practicality advanced by retailers. The variety of temperature control provisions contained in these directives is inconsistent with the risk assessment (HACCP), approach set out in the General Hygiene Directive; and the variety of different temperatures specified in the product specific directives is unnecessarily bureaucratic.

The temperature regime set out in the UK Food Hygiene Regulations (1995) establishes a simpler regime requiring food to be kept at a temperature assessed on a risk analysis basis, with a fallback position of 8°C. We support this approach. The goal-based nature of the 1995 Food Hygiene Regulations is more in step with modern retail practices than with the current EU provisions.

We recommend that the Vertical Directives be abolished. The few areas where it may be useful to retain specific procedures, for example oysters, which must be kept in tanks, should be put into annexes to the General Hygiene Directive.

A major difficulty we face with deregulation in the food business is that so much of it is dominated by the EC requirements. However, we must not take this as an excuse for not being able to make changes.

The Ministry of Agriculture, Fisheries and Food (MAFF) has taken a very positive approach and has tried hard to address some of the issues, but inevitably progress is slow. In recent years we have made progress in a greater understanding about implementation of EU Directives. One helpful change has been to ensure that commencement dates provide some flexibility to ease the cost of change. This is particularly the case in food labelling. Making sure that these changes are grouped with quarterly start dates rather than the dates determined by the Directives themselves has been helpful. But the key to the future is a wider acceptance that new regulation should meet consistent criteria (see Figure 2).

Figure 2
Criteria for regulation

1. Do not interfere for the sake of it - remember the umbrella.

2. Do not think that the regulatory response is the only one you can make when faced with a problem

3. If you have to regulate then: (a) make it goal-based; (b) think of its impact on small business; (c) keep it in proportion

4. Make sure the regulations can be applied in practice and are fairly enforced.

These are some of the criteria I would offer. There is nothing very remarkable about them but what is remarkable is the unwillingness of some politicians and regulators to adopt them.

To close may I make some comments on battles that are still being fought - prospective candidates seem to me to be as follows:
- EU Compositional Standards
- EU Vertical Hygiene Directives
- EU Produce Marketing Standards
- Ensuring that changes to labelling are phased in over manageable length of time.
- Liquor Licensing
- Game Licensing

EU compositional standards
These were initially seen as a precursor to the free movement of goods within the single market, but these quality standards have fallen into disrepute. They are restrictive, protectionist and stifle innovation. Compositional standards have become a blunt instrument in consumer protection; retailers would prefer to see them replaced by an approach based on the Quantitative Ingredient Declaration (QUID) labelling (see CEC, 1997). The Commission's move to introduce QUID is welcome

and we look forward to playing an active role in helping MAFF produce the relevant guidance notes.

Liquor licences
This is a frustrating saga. Recently, the Home Office issued new draft regulations on the procedures for granting and holding liquor licences and said that these would save business more than £4 million a year. Whilst this is to be welcomed, the plans announced are nowhere near as radical as those put forward in the consultation document which themselves were based on the recommendations of a Home Office Working Party on Licence Transfers. In fact, it is difficult to recognise the draft order as stemming from the consultation document published in July 1996.

Game licences
The license dates from 1931 when poaching was rife. Now most game is farmed or imported. The license no longer serves a useful purpose. All Sainsbury's venison is farmed and under the livestock agreement which we have with our suppliers there are provisions for dealing with the traceability of game. This license is out of date and we recommend it should be abolished.

CONCLUSION
I do not think that anything I have said this morning is revolutionary. It is certainly nothing that has not already been said once if not many times before. Even when the political will is there, as I believe it is at least in this country, to alleviate the burdens on business without undermining public confidence in food safety, the practice is a long, hard slog with many frustrations. Nevertheless, the Deregulation and Contracting Out Act (1994) provides a mechanism which may yet have a long-lasting impact on the way regulations are made.

REFERENCES
CEC (1992) *The Sutherland Report. The internal market after 1992 - meeting the challenge. Report to the European Commission by the high level group on the operation of the internal market.* SEC (92) 2277. Brussels: CEC.
CEC (1995) *The Monitor Report. Report of the group of independent experts on legislative and administrative simplification.* COM (95) 288 final/2. Brussels: CEC.
CEC (1997) *Amending Directive 79/112/EEC on the approximation of the laws of the Member States relating to the labelling, presentation and advertising of foodstuffs.* COM 97/4/EC. Brussels: CEC.

Marshall BJ & Miller FA (Eds)(1997) *Management of regulation in the food chain - balancing costs, benefits and effects.*
CAS Paper 36. Reading: Centre for Agricultural Strategy.

4 Regulations and the catering industry

Colin Andrews

Discovery, they say, consists of looking at the same thing as everyone else and thinking something different. It was therefore with some trepidation that I accepted this challenge of attempting to offer a concerted view on regulation, and its effects on such a diverse industry as catering. Catering services are an essential requirement across the whole spectrum of private- and public-sector businesses and organisations; in no particular order of precedence of their value to the country's economy, they range from hotel and restaurant chains to rail, ship and aircraft catering; to industrial, local authority, hospitals and schools catering; to large and small independent restaurants and cafés; to outside and functions catering; and to fish-and-chip shops, take-aways, and fast-food and sandwich bars - all these comprise the vitally important catering sector of the food chain.

The establishment and implementation of rules and regulations designed to ensure the provision of safe food throughout this enormous business are very difficult indeed. The vast majority of caterers in this country are very proud of what has been achieved over the last decade in the improvements in real standards of the millions of meals being served. Because of the increase of foreign travel and the change in consumers' perception of and desire for different and quality food, the achievement is nothing short of a revolution. Some of the very best food in the world can now be eaten in Britain, whether it be traditional British dishes, or those that have been improved and enriched by the influences from the rest of Europe, the near and far East, and from across the Atlantic.

No-one in their right mind who operates any form of catering establishment, would set out to offer food for sale which is, as it says in The Food Safety Act 1990 'Not of the nature and substance demanded'. The industry has therefore taken the whole problem of planning and procedures necessary for the preparation and service not only of quality food, but also of safe food, very seriously indeed. Considerable time and money has been spent by the leading organisations in the industry in publishing their own guidelines for their members and, in many cases, producing a specific document as a basis of self-regulation which far exceeds the requirements of the law, or existing or proposed European Commission directives. Unfortunately the influence of those guidelines tends to be limited to the larger companies, or the companies supplying them.

A large group of hotels or restaurants can afford to, or maybe believe they cannot afford not to, appoint a senior person to establish a policy and a department to implement it, designed to ensure that everyone carries out procedures that will offer safe food. That senior officer will probably represent the company on one or more of the catering industry associations, and will have the time and opportunity to consider and contribute to the formulation of regulations and proposals for deregulation. As far as the larger organisations are concerned, I believe that the current regulations, supplemented by codes of practice which in many respects are even more rigorous, are being adhered to and successfully maintain the safety of our food.

But what of the medium- or small-business operators? They too are very proud of the quality of their products and their reputation. They know that if the price and quality are right, they will be commercially successful. But they have also realised that just to buy the best quality products from reputable suppliers, and to prepare, cook and serve food in clean premises is not enough. They know, if only from coverage in the media, that things can go wrong even in the best establishments. They therefore need to show due diligence in case they should inadvertently have a problem and they know that situations will inevitably arise in which they may need help. They can either study what 'hazard analysis' and 'due diligence' means to them, taking time and costing them money; they can appoint a consultant, costing them even more money but seen by most as probably the best solution; or they can call in their local Environmental Health Officer (EHO).

The problem is that the industry still abounds with stories, some apocryphal and some not, of EHOs walking into premises unannounced, as they have a right to do, and causing chaos. There is one about a restaurateur taking the right approach, bringing in his EHO at an early stage, and planning with his complete approval, a kitchen to the highest specification, which included plastic seamless wall finishes. On completion of the work several months later, he rang the EHO only to be told that he had moved on and had been replaced by a new EHO. Imagine then the restaurateur's surprise when the new man said on inspection that he did not approve of plastic walling, and it would have to be stripped off so that he could see what it was covering up - fortunately the restaurateur had the original approval in writing. Apocryphal or not, the very existence of such stories creates an atmosphere of distrust.

The EHO is in an unenviable position, being both advisor and policeman, and let me say now, that EHOs and their associations have worked extremely hard over the last couple of years to avoid incidents such as the one I have just related. When talking to EHOs, they tell me that their territories are so large that the number of visits they can make are very much restricted; their responsibilities are furthermore very diverse, covering all sorts of health-related activities in their area, and they therefore have very little time in which to concentrate on food, and certainly no time to establish a relationship with all the caterers in their local authority area. Ideally, a close working relationship between EHOs and caterers would enable the former to act as respected and valuable advisors. If the responsible caterer is asked for his opinion on regulation and legislation he will say that provided the rules are simple and achievable, they will be embraced as part of his overall policy; and that the need for policing is readily recognised and accepted, because there will always be some 'scallywag' down the road who will ignore all the regulations and 'do things on the cheap'.

To sum up I believe that the catering industry genuinely considers it is, for the most part, providing high quality, safe food; and it feels rightly or wrongly, that it is far more heavily regulated than its counterparts in other countries in the European Union. It is very easy for politicians to be moved to knee-jerk reactions, to safeguard, as they see it, the consumers' interest, and incidents such as those we have experienced and read about in recent months must be taken very seriously indeed. But many incidents are totally distorted by sensational media coverage. We strongly believe that sufficient regulations must be in place to ensure that safe food can be produced and also that guidelines on how to achieve standards that ensure compliance are also in place. The very large majority of responsible companies are following them, but I would like to propose several pointers that will help to get information over to the rest of the industry and thus make sure that they include safe procedures as part of their daily routine:

- Environmental Health Departments need more people who are better trained in the intricacies of food processing and preparation so that they can gain the respect and cooperation of caterers, and develop an advisory role that can be even more effective than resorting to enforcement;
- training grants should be available so that every caterer feels he can afford to have all of his staff trained in safe food practices. It is not at the top where incidents start, it is usually the ignorance of a junior member of the staff that causes problems;

- a system that provides continuing distribution of information direct to the caterer is required since not every caterer can afford the time or money to belong to an association;
- every effort must be made to avoid more prescriptive forms of regulation; there are already sufficient regulations and guidelines in operation which will, provided they are simple, clear, and understandable, ensure that the catering industry at all levels will provide safe food to its consuming public.

DISCUSSION

Professor Alan Malcolm (Director of the Institute of Food Research) commented that food safety is not just about microbiological safety - there are a number of people who suffer from allergic reactions or intolerance to food in one way or another. He therefore asked the speaker for his views on the ways in which the catering industry can take on board the necessity for getting information to consumers in catering outlets on this important issue.

Mr Colin Andrews, in reply, accepted the importance of such advice and stressed that to have the necessary impact it should go direct to the caterers themselves. He felt that it would be difficult for Local Authorities to identify every caterer in their area and he instanced cases where caterers, through lack of information and guidance, had unwittingly included ingredients that had caused problems and had undeservedly received unfavourable press comment. He, nevertheless, felt that if through appropriate Government policies and funding, the necessary knowledge and advice could be disseminated to all in the business of catering, then a favourable response from the industry would follow.

Marshall BJ & Miller FA (Eds)(1997) *Management of regulation in the food chain - balancing costs, benefits and effects.*
CAS Paper 36. Reading: Centre for Agricultural Strategy.

5 The food manufacturers' perspective

Guy Walker

INTRODUCTION

I am delighted to have been invited to give the manufacturers' perspective on the important issues under discussion here today. Let me begin by stressing that the food industry needs effective, sensible regulation. Properly enforced, such a regulatory framework should ensure consumer confidence in the safety of our products and provide for fair competition. Safety is the paramount concern of our industry. No responsible producer wishes to jeopardise his relationship with his customers by providing unsafe or sub-standard products. Nor does he wish to believe that less scrupulous competitors, who have no such concerns, could enter the market and undermine his good work.

So good regulation is vital to the industry. The question is: what constitutes good regulation? How can we best ensure consumer protection without undermining the competitiveness of the industry, an industry which employs some half a million people and accounts for over 16% of gross manufacturing output in the United Kingdom (UK)? How can we ensure that an industry that offers consumers a wider range of safe, nutritious, wholesome and affordable foods than ever before is able to continue to do so?

PRINCIPLES OF GOOD REGULATION

It is the Food and Drink Federation (FDF)'s view that this can only be done by ensuring that five principles are applied throughout the regulatory process, from the earliest consideration of a draft proposal to the enforcement of enacted legislation.

NEED FOR REGULATION

First, regulations should only be considered if they are objectively necessary for consumer protection or to ensure fair trade. If there is no problem, or no benefit from regulating, then do not consider them. This does not simply apply to food law, of course, but to all areas of legislation affecting industrial competitiveness. The proposed European Union (EU) regulations for labelling beef and beef products are a case in point. Detailed Community labelling rules are already rigorously enforced by Trading Standards Officers to ensure that no false claims are made about products. All the proposed regulations would do is make it more difficult for companies to respond to consumer concerns by insisting that labelling of beef and beef products is subject to an inevitably slow process of prior approval.

CONTENT

Secondly, any measures subsequently proposed must be proportional to the need or problem identified. In broad terms, FDF welcomes the Government's presumption in favour of goal-based rather than prescriptive regulations. This is certainly the way forward in the area of food hygiene, for example, where clear principles and objectives should be set down in legislation applicable throughout the food chain. Tools such as HACCP (Hazard Analysis and Critical Control Points) can then be applied by companies to ensure that their particular operating methods result in products that are consistently safe. I stress the point that food hygiene rules must apply, and be adequately enforced, along the whole of the food chain.

Food safety is primarily a matter of scientific fact. In order to establish the facts, however, it is vital that there is a properly-funded programme of public research to underpin the work carried out by the industry itself. Other aspects of food legislation, such as the question of what constitutes adequate consumer information, are more subjective. FDF supports the provision of clear, understandable and meaningful information to enable consumers to make informed purchases when choosing food. But rules need to be sufficiently detailed and unambiguous, though, of course, practical and proportionate, in order to prevent widely differing interpretations as to what is acceptable both within the UK and across the Single Market.

We have to accept that legislation resulting from late-night political compromise in Brussels, the source of the vast majority of legislation specifically affecting the food industry, is frequently unclear as to its practical application. Widely differing interpretations are often possible. Where appropriate, the industry would therefore appreciate EU and/or UK guidelines - for example on the recently agreed amendment to the labelling rules under EC Directive 97/4 requiring

Quantitative Ingredient Declaration (QUID). If QUID is to work at all, common definitions of ingredients and common quantification techniques will be essential. The costs incurred by industry in having to change packaging and reformulate products in order to meet differing interpretations by various enforcement authorities would seriously impede competitiveness. Such changes would also confuse consumers, who ultimately have to bear the costs.

INNOVATION
It is, however, equally important that regulations are flexible enough to allow for innovation: this is my third principle. The history of the food and drink industry has been the development of evermore sophisticated products and production techniques providing consumers with an ever-wider choice of tasty, nutritious and convenient products at prices that are affordable. Consumer choice will be restricted and the industry's international competitiveness will suffer if industry is not allowed to respond innovatively to new technologies. The laborious process of obtaining amendments to the Directives on Miscellaneous Additives, Sweeteners and Colours is a case in point. Safety concerns must of course be met, but there must be workable fast-track procedures to enable the industry to respond adequately to the needs of the market and technological progress.

Similarly, in view of consumer interest in healthy eating and so-called functional foods (is there not a better name for these 'designer' products?), manufacturers should be allowed to make health claims for their products where scientifically justifiable. Such claims would be controlled by enforcement authorities as is the case with other food legislation. Modern biotechnology is another area of innovation that could bring substantial consumer benefits. There are strict procedures in place for ensuring that genetically-modified foods are safe. The potential benefits in the form of reduced wastage, and enhanced disease and pest resistance are colossal, and could translate into lower prices and improved products for consumers if allowed to develop.

CONSULTATION
Fourthly, regulations must be subject to full consultation with all interested parties at the earliest opportunity and throughout their subsequent passage to law. Proper representation and involvement of manufacturers, consumers and other interested parties should encourage open and informed debate to ensure that an appropriate balance of interests ensues. Measures such as Compliance Cost Assessments and increased use of risk assessment are a step forward. However, all too frequently they are too little too late. In any case, the

effectiveness and accuracy of industry assessments of compliance costs must depend on receiving a full explanation of the practical effect of the proposed legislation. Even then, costs can be difficult to quantify. So much depends on implementation and second-stage detailed rules. Costs may be hidden if reformulation is undertaken anyway, or if legislation has been pre-empted, or if future activity is circumscribed by inflexible regulations that discourage innovation. As an example of the sorts of difficulties that can face the industry, QUID will not simply involve changes to labels: it will require detailed records to be kept.

It is important to bear in mind that such costs are not borne simply by the industry. They have implications for prices to consumers, and for jobs and investment. They affect all businesses, small and large. Whilst, on occasion, there may be a case for derogations for smaller businesses, the economy will suffer if larger businesses, who are key investors, are routinely discriminated against. And in some areas, such as food safety, it makes no sense at all to apply looser rules to smaller businesses. The key is to ensure that in all instances costs are measured carefully against benefits accruing, to ensure that society enjoys a net benefit.

IMPLEMENTATION AND ENFORCEMENT

Fifthly, regulations must be uniformly implemented and enforced, within the UK and across the EU. The Commission estimates that only 56% of its Single Market measures have been implemented in every Member State. Delays and poor implementation prevent businesses from fully exploiting the potential of the Single Market as much as over-zealous implementation (better known as 'gold-plating'). Infringement proceedings taken by the Commission take too long and appear to have little effect, allowing Member States to continue to shield their own industries from competition. Redress *via* the courts is rarely a viable option for an individual company. The industry looks to vigorous commitment to a properly functioning Single Market in Westminster and Brussels. Such commitment should also tackle uneven enforcement of EU legislation, widely regarded as the most persistent barrier to trade and fair competition within the Single Market. As we have seen all too clearly in the European response to the Bovine Spongiform Encephalopathy (BSE) crisis, the Single Market depends on mutual confidence in enforcement in Member States. If the price for this is increased market surveillance and audit of each Member State's enforcement procedures and activities by the Commission, then it may well be a price worth paying.

Within the UK, the industry has generally enjoyed good relations with enforcement authorities. However, occasional overzealous and inconsistent enforcement has long been a 'bugbear'. Enforcement must be adequately resourced to deter bad practice along the length of the food chain. It must not, however, be unduly onerous on the law-abiding. The performance of enforcement authorities should be measured by the degree of compliance with legislation, rather than the number of prosecutions. System-based enforcement, where inspection is based on risk, should help to focus activity where it is most needed. Consumer protection is enhanced by preventive enforcement of this kind, whereby the emphasis is put on helping companies to comply with what are often extremely complex regulations. Prevention must be better than cure. I should, however, mention that there is concern within the industry that some of the unitary authorities arising from the Local Government Review may be too small to allow for adequate resourcing and training of enforcement bodies.

FDF still believes that prosecution is too often used too quickly by some authorities, and welcomes the Model Appeals Mechanism and the business-friendly enforcement provisions introduced under the Deregulation and Contracting Out Act 1994. These provisions should help spread best enforcement practice resulting in fairer, more transparent and more consistent enforcement across the board.

UK GOVERNMENT DEREGULATION INITIATIVE
It should be clear from what I have said that FDF supports the principle behind the Government's deregulation initiative, and welcomes much of the work of the Deregulation Task Force. However, the Federation will not support any deregulatory proposals that could compromise consumer safety. Nor could we be expected to support any proposals that would undermine the competitive position of our own industry. It is also important that when consulting on proposals for deregulation on food the Government takes into account the views of *all* sectors of the industry. One instance where this did not happen was the reduction of temperature controls for chilled foods from five to eight degrees centigrade.

Having said that we support the deregulation initiative in principle, I wonder if I could make one small plea to Government. Change its name: 'deregulation' is a misnomer. As I said at the beginning, what we need is simpler legislation that is fair and workable, not its complete removal. Not only is the name inaccurate, but the dread word 'deregulation' frightens consumers as well as our colleagues in Europe.

ACTION IN EUROPE
And if we are to have good regulation, we need to convince other Member States of the merits of our case. As I said earlier, much of the

legislation affecting the food and drink industry is derived from Brussels. FDF asks the Government to continue to make the case in Europe for a regulatory framework that imposes burdens on the industry only when they are objectively necessary for consumer protection or fair trade. Such regulations must be consistently and equitably implemented and similarly enforced across the EU.

FDF was pleased to see the publication recently of guidelines for Ministers *Good regulatory principles and practice in Europe* (see Deregulation Unit, Cabinet Office, 1997). The Federation was similarly encouraged by the Commission's adoption of internal guidelines for better law-making and by its recent report to Council and the European Parliament on the pilot phase of its initiative entitled Simpler Legislation for the Internal Market which goes under the appropriate acronym of SLIM (see CEC 1996). We look forward to the Commission's response to the Council's call for the extension of the application of SLIM to other areas of legislation. We also welcome the emphasis on a properly-functioning and competitive Single Market in M Santer's Confidence Pact for Employment in Europe.

But 'the proof of the pudding is in the eating'. I have to say that all the words and good intentions on the subject of simpler regulation have as yet had very little practical effect in our industry. We are still confronted with a mass of complex, inconsistent, often unjustifiable regulations that make our job more difficult and serve no consumer protection purpose. How much information can be required on a food label, for example, before the print size becomes so small that it is rendered unintelligible?!

We very much hope that the long-awaited Commission Green Paper on Food Law will address the need for consistency, proportionality and simplification, as well as other important issues such as the need to extend product liability along the whole length of the food chain. Consideration will also need to be given to M Santer's proposal to bring food safety policy at European level under the Commission's Consumer Affairs Directorate. It may be that the legislative process itself needs to be reviewed to ensure both maximum accountability and efficiency of decision-taking and high quality and consistent regulations. It is to be hoped that the opportunity to consider this will be taken during the Inter-Governmental Conference.

UK FOOD AGENCY

Finally, I know that many are interested in FDF's views on calls for a UK Food Agency. We have been following the debate very closely. If the industry is to be able to meet the expectations of its customers, there is no doubt that Government must play its part. Consumers must have confidence in the administrative structures established by Government to monitor, regulate and promote the industry, and in the adequacy of publicly-funded research. That confidence is, I regret to say, waning rapidly. The Government's recent announcement on the establishment of a Food Safety Council and an independent Food Safety Adviser can therefore be welcomed as one small step towards that goal.

The announcement has further fuelled discussions on the mechanisms that will ensure both consumer protection and industry competitiveness. The key issue must be to ensure both an appropriate balance of interests and representation in the development and implementation of policy and effective enforcement of standards along the whole of the food chain. And this view has been pretty well reflected throughout the wide range of reactions from the industry, media and other interests. The National Farmers' Union has identified transparency as the highest priority. The Consumers' Association has expressed concerns about the effective powers of the proposed Council, a view shared, it seems, by the SAFE (Sustainable Agriculture, Food and Environment) Alliance. My own view, and that of the Federation, echoes that of the Financial Times: the Government's proposals are fine - as far as they go. But are they enough? It is not simply a question of advice, but effective implementation of that advice. Whether this can be achieved under the Government's proposals, or whether it requires a new body, is clearly provoking a useful and interesting debate and one to which we must speedily find the correct outcome.

REFERENCES

CEC (1996) *Simpler legislation for the internal market (SLIM): a pilot project.* COM (96)204 final. Brussels: CEC.

CEC (1997) *Amending Directive 79/112/EEC on the approximation of the laws of the Member States relating to the labelling, presentation and advertising of foodstuffs.* COM 97/4/EC.

Deregulation Unit, Cabinet Office (1997) *Good regulatory principles and practice in Europe.* London: The Stationery Office.

Marshall BJ & Miller FA (Eds)(1997) *Management of regulation in the food chain - balancing costs, benefits and effects.* CAS Paper 36. Reading: Centre for Agricultural Strategy.

6 Science, technology and research related to food crops

Geraldine Schofield

What I would like to do today is to describe in a little detail, the technological developments in science, technology, and research related to food crops, in order to set the context for regulatory developments. I think it is important that we understand what is happening in this field of research. I do not propose to go into the science too deeply, but I think that an overview would be useful. As somebody mentioned this morning, the method of bringing any innovation to market comprises a very complex series of interactions - it is not simple and there are a lot of stages involved (see Figure 1).

Figure 1
The techno-economic network

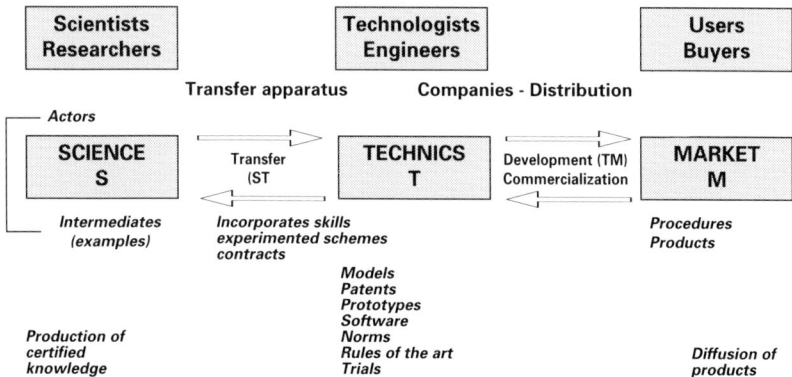

Source: Adapted from Callan *et al* (1992)

The network seen here comprises scientists, researchers, technologists, engineers, users, and buyers. It is, I think, widely acknowledged that the gap between a 'technological push', where we are looking at technology leading development, and a 'market pull' where the market is demanding and expanding, has actually narrowed over the last twenty or thirty years. Market demand can also orientate the technology. Innovations which really mobilise scientific results and technological skills are the result of numerous interactions between researchers, engineers, marketing people and regulators and, of course, the consumers. All of these developments are a complex series of iterations, negotiations and compromises in order to get the technology into the market place.

With reference to food crops, what are the new technologies? What are we delivering now and what can we expect? It has already been mentioned a couple of times today, that one of the major areas will be in the development and use of biotechnology. I am talking about this in the broadest sense of the word. What we need to do is to set today's science in the context of agricultural developments, traditional plant breeding and developments in food processing (see Figure 2).

Figure 2
Biotechnology - in context

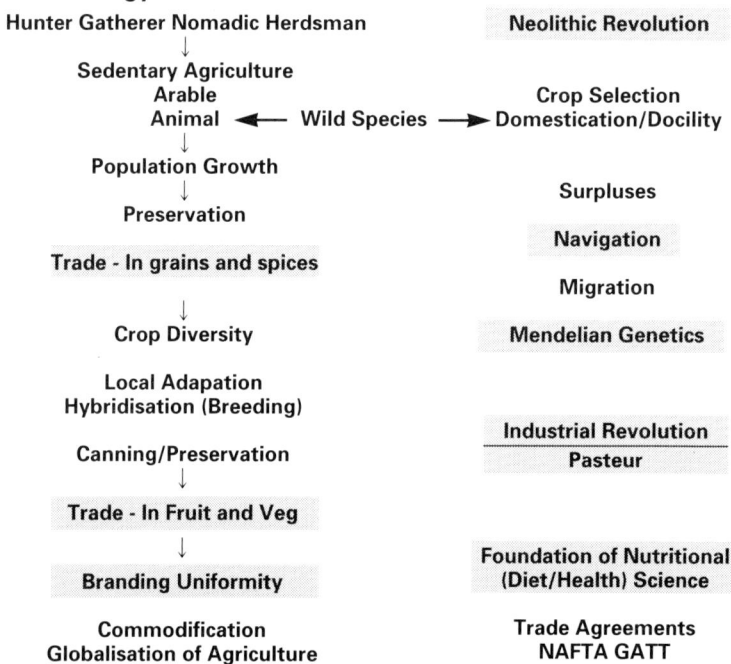

Source: Schofield (1997)

As can be seen this figure takes us a long way back in history. We really need to understand where we come from and where we are going and one of the important things I would like to stress at this stage is, as indicated at the bottom of the figure, the importance of 'commodification' and the globalisation of agriculture which, when you think of regulating and safety issues, could be a major factor in the changes which will take place. We also have trade agreements such as the North American Free Trade Agreement (NAFTA) and the General Agreement on Tariffs and Trade (GATT), which may come into play if we choose to ban certain imports or specify how we import from the United States (US) and other countries and how we export to other countries.

As outlined here, the position we have reached now is largely a product of trial and error. Before the introduction of new varieties into the food chain or into the environment, there were no regulatory structures and no legal hurdles such as those we have now. The production of new varieties of food crops (we currently have a narrow range of about twenty) and the expansion of varieties depends, to some extent, on the origin of the crop - where it was domesticated, the centre of genetic diversity, and so on. Therefore the application of the new science of gene technology, together with our understanding of the wild species and the genetic make-up of crops, open up options for improving varieties, providing alternatives to traditional food processes, and, hopefully, to the sensitive and sensible management of ecosystems in agriculture. If I can just remind you of what we are talking about in terms of genetic modification (see Figure 3), it is possible to enhance variation through genetic modification.

Figure 3
Three ways of enhancing variation through genetic modification

- **Multiplication or blocking genes already present in a cell**

- **Transfer of gene between organisms**

- **Modification of DNA sequence to produce required product/ product with modified properties**

Source: Schofield (1997)

However, genetic modification is only one way. Transgenic plants will not replace conventional plant breeding overnight; and I am not going to tell you that modern biotechnology is the same as traditional biotechnology - it is not. However, new genetic technologies can assist in breeding: technologies for breeding systems using genetics as analytical tools not manipulative tools.

I would like to turn now to some of the key topics in plant biotechnology (see Figure 4) and draw attention to what is actually happening out there, in terms of genetics, plant breeding and gene mapping.

Figure 4
Key topics in plant biotechnology

TOPIC	AREAS OF RESEARCH
Genetics and Breeding	- Genome Research - Gene Mapping - Genetic markers in breeding

Plant Development	- Structure
	  (height, branching, leaves, roots)
	- Flowers
	  (structure, colour, timing of flowering)
	- Hybrid production
	  (self incompatibility; male sterility)

Altering Inputs and Yields	- Herbicide resistance in food and non-food crops - Insect resistance in food and non-food crops - Resistance to bacterial, fungal and viral diseases - Nitrogen fixation in non-legumes - Photosynthetic efficiency improvement

Products and Applications	- Sugar
	- Starch
	  (different composition or higher content)
	- Oils
	  (different composition or higher content)
	- Flavours and fragrances
	  (in food or as extracts)
	- Speciality organic compounds (colours)
	- Storage proteins
	- Fruit (ripening and quality)

Environment	- Drought, salt and heat tolerance - Flood tolerance - Cold adaption (extending growing limits) - Frost resistance (specifically against freezing)

Source: Schofield (1997)

I am sure you have heard all about these areas of work on plant development relating to structure, height and flowering, and also altering yields and inputs, which I will come to later in more detail. The two big developments we are seeing coming through at the moment are on herbicide and insect resistance. The developments of particular interest to the food processors are: compositional (eg, on sugars and starches for instance); health benefits from different oils, flavours, special organic compounds; storage proteins and fruit ripening quality. There are also potential benefits from being able to grow crop plants in unfavourable environmental conditions, and use plants for industrial rather than food use.

The process of developments leading to the marketing of biotechnology-derived products can be divided into three phases (see Figure 5).

Figure 5
Three phases of entry of plant biotechnology into the market

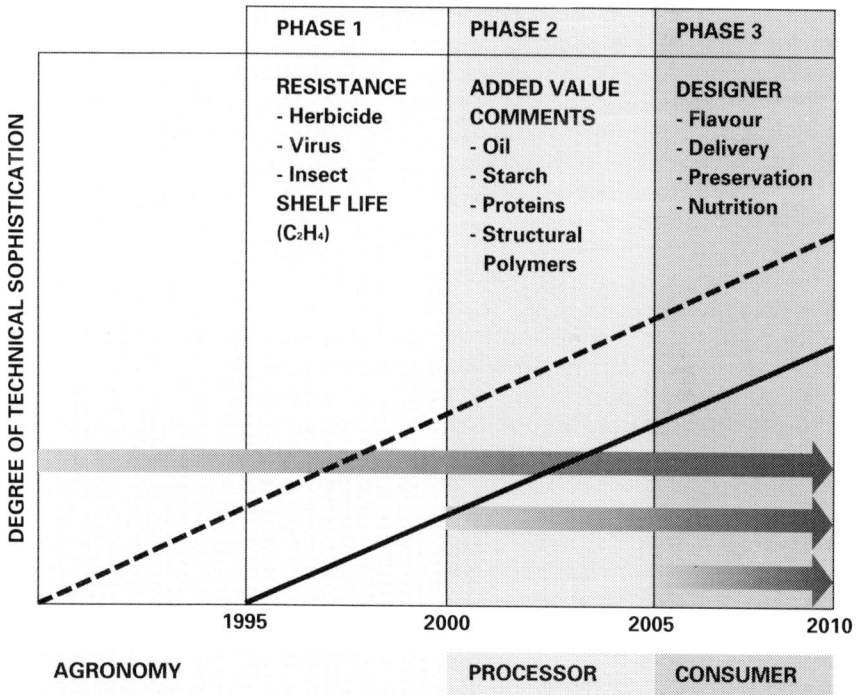

	PHASE 1	PHASE 2	PHASE 3
	RESISTANCE	ADDED VALUE	DESIGNER
	- Herbicide	COMMENTS	- Flavour
	- Virus	- Oil	- Delivery
	- Insect	- Starch	- Preservation
	SHELF LIFE	- Proteins	- Nutrition
	(C_2H_4)	- Structural	
		Polymers	

DEGREE OF TECHNICAL SOPHISTICATION

1995   2000   2005   2010

AGRONOMY   PROCESSOR   CONSUMER

Source: Schofield (1997)

At the moment, most crop plants derived *via* gene technology are for agronomic purposes. They are mainly commodity crops that can be traded on the world market. They are of no benefit *directly* for the processor or for the consumer - it is purely an agronomic trait, although there are environmental benefits. The next phase we are looking forward to is added-value major commodities, such as oil and starch proteins. And, finally, we are hoping to deliver functionality, that is more nutritious foods, more flavour and taste, almost designer foods - but that is some way off. The degree of technical sophistication required actually increases as we go through these phases. On the figure, the *dotted* line refers to technology, and the *continuous* line is where we see products coming to market and, as previously mentioned, we already have herbicide- and insect-resistant crops in the fields. Indeed, in North America this year there are probably several million hectares of transgenic plants.

One of the questions is obviously the safety of these crops, but it is not just the safety as Sheila McKechnie mentioned this morning - it is other issues such as informing the consumer by labelling. We need to decide what we are going to label and how to do it to achieve effective results. Consideration must also be given to the sort of legal framework that must be devised for these developments in order to provide information for consumers who may have ethical or other concerns about this technology. This is apart from the safety issues - but safety is paramount. The potential production of genetically-modified organisms has already produced an avalanche of legislation to control the technology. I will not go through a lot of detail, but we have already seen a great deal of legislation since the introduction of gene technology back in the laboratory stages in the early 1970s in the United Kingdom and in North America, and more recently in the past five or six years, legislation arising from the European Union (EU). As was mentioned earlier today by Angela Browning, when we are addressing the issues of food crops and regulation, it is not just an end product that we have to regulate - we have to take it all the way back in the innovation process and there are many stages involved in getting new plant varieties, maybe genetically-modified varieties, onto the market. If I now go back to Figure 1 this helps to explain what is happening. Consumer acceptance and consumer feedback are going to feed this technological cycle. I mentioned that we do have regulation, indeed there is extensive regulation certainly in the field testing that covers laboratory trials, greenhouse containment trials, and small-scale field trials, all of which are regulated in the EU. The EU regulations were, however, probably introduced much later than they should have been. In some cases I think they have set back the European industry at the expense of developments in the US simply because when they came out they were too late and too prescriptive.

The production of transgenic plants and the creation of appropriate legislation poses major difficulties and challenges for legislators, and for industry and scientists. Biotechnology, looked at it in its broadest sense, is a set of dynamic innovating tools - they can be pulled off the shelf and used, and any legal framework has to understand and try and cope with very fast innovation in this area. So it is not easy, either for the regulators themselves, or for industry that sees competitive advantage in using these innovatory tools. I would say that, at this stage, the 'precautionary principle' is the correct one. We do have appropriate regulations in place in terms of environmental hazard as well as hazard to human health. We also have regulation in relation to what is happening in terms of food processing and, during the last month, we have seen the introduction of a Novel Foods Regulation in Europe. One of the problems with that, of course, is that we really still do not have a definition of what is 'novel' (and how long novel will remain novel), or what is 'equivalent' with respect to conventional foods and traditional breeding techniques. We are, I am afraid, back in the area of risk assessment and risk-based approaches and, once again, we will see, probably in the media, debates among scientists over what is meant by risk and whether something is 'safe' or not. This is likely to include issues of environmental safety as well as human health and safety.

A major question now is how we push forward a risk-based approach to ensure safety, and, at the same time, allow innovation and industrial competitiveness to go ahead: this is certainly not going to be easy to achieve. A brief mention was made earlier about what happened in the US where they have taken a somewhat different approach based on the competitiveness of their own industry. One of the problems that we have at the moment in terms of regulation and importation, particularly relating to transgenics, is the question of the enormous imports of commodity crops into Europe. How do we actually regulate them if we are all saying we regulate them on the basis of safety? If we make the assumption they are safe, we still have a huge problem, particularly with this technology, of how to inform people about what is going on in an area that is extremely complex scientifically, and where these commodity products are likely to be incorporated into almost every processed product on the supermarket shelf.

So, in order to use this technology, and benefit from it, there are major questions not only of implementing regulation, but also of ensuring that we actually have customer feedback - which tells us whether the consumer feels at home with the technology and feels that it is safe - in order to make sure the innovatory cycle is closed. Biotechnology is an innovatory tool, and the food industry is interested in innovation in the same way as other industries, and hopefully this technology can go forward. But what we need are continuing revisions of risk and the legislative framework. I think it was Thomas Jefferson who said 'laws and regulations must go hand in hand with the development of the human mind' and that means applying the knowledge we have learnt into this area, and getting the regulatory structures correct so that we can use this technology to everybody's advantage.

REFERENCE

Callan, M, Laredo, P, Rabelauson, V, Gonard, T, Cheroy, T (1992) Management of technological programs and the dynamics of techno-economic networks. The case of the AFME. *Research Policy* 21, 215-236.

DISCUSSION

Mr George Douglas (Farmer and Bristol University Agriculture Committee) expressed interest in the regulatory aspects of technology research, but felt that the one subject not covered was the question of yield. The basic responsibility we all have is to feed the world, and there are two things that are going to stop that. One is the emphasis placed on ethics, a 'science' which no-one really understands - and the other is world patent law as it stands at the moment. The World Trade Organisation is probably the only organisation capable of developing patent law in ways that clarify confusions arising from existing world patents and local patents - it is therefore vitally important to the movement forward of biotechnological science that these matters are addressed in a commonsense way.

Dr Schofield agreed that the patent situation is very difficult because until four or five years ago, the European Patent Office was not really very *au fait* with this subject. However, following pressure for a European Directive on patents, it now looks as if the European Patent Office has 'got its act together' though it appears that the Biotechnology Inventions Directive may actually hinder some of the patenting that we already have and will be negative in relation to competition with the US. Dr Schofield also saw the question of farmers' and breeders' plant variety rights as a huge issue and felt that whilst the process of resolving the problems is not likely to stop the role of innovation in the science and technology, a lot of difficulty seems inevitable when biotechnology patents have to be incorporated with plant variety rights.

Marshall BJ & Miller FA (Eds)(1997) *Management of regulation in the food chain - balancing costs, benefits and effects.*
CAS Paper 36. Reading: Centre for Agricultural Strategy.

7 Regulations and small food and agriculture businesses

Robert Robertson

IINTRODUCTION

I much appreciate this opportunity to express, as Chairman of the Agriculture Committee of the Federation of Small Businesses (FSB), the viewpoints and concerns of the small firms engaged in the production, processing and manufacture of food on the impact of regulations. We have to understand and comply with the same range of complex regulatory measures as those running the large businesses with the obvious disadvantage of fewer resources; food producers in particular cannot pass on the costs of compliance with regulation in their prices since they have to accept the prices that the market offers.

With the increasing number of people working in the small firms' sector, and the ever-changing basis of legislation, health and safety is a major area of concern. Despite the Government's stated commitment to deregulation, we still have a constant stream of new legislation, much of it due to European directives, over which we appear to have little control. The theme I wish to address today therefore is that 'complex regulations are self-defeating - and that there is a need for reversal of the trend and simplification'.

May I set the scene with a few relevant quotes, references and comments. The front page of *The Independent* of 3 December 1996 reports a dramatic rise in the number of *Escherichia coli* incidents in England and Wales in recent years from 53 cases in 1985 to 1046 in 1996 (see Figure 1). The same paper on 17 January 1997 reports '*E. coli* death toll rivals world's worst food poisoning'; and in 1994 the Communicable Disease Surveillance Centre estimated food poisoning as costing £1Billion per annum. With each food scare, whether it is

E. coli, Bovine Spongiform Encephalopathy (BSE), Creutzfeldt-Jacob Disease (CJD), *Salmonella* or whatever, we have the same routine. Firstly, hysterical media calls for more regulation, then Government commissioning an academic study, followed by ill-conceived new rules, licenses etc, the cost of which devastates many small businesses by cutting their hours available for production and tempting the cutting of corners on simple hygiene practices. In other words, too much legislation is self-defeating.

Figure 1
Rise of *Escherichia coli* cases

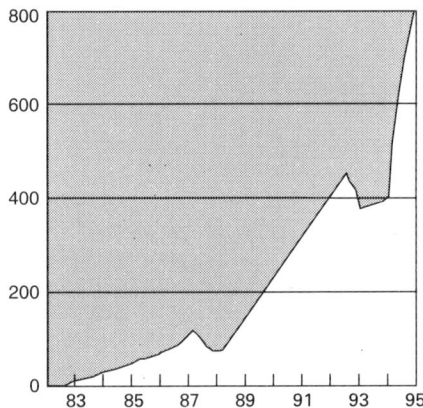

Source: *The Independent,* 3 December 1996

Mr Hugh Morrison, Director of the Scotch Whisky Association, when faced with a bizarre battery of new legislation, said in an interview recently reported in the *Sunday Telegraph*: 'The trouble is, we live today in a 'play safe culture'. No sooner does someone conjure up even the faintest possibility of some 'risk' than the bureaucracy lumbers into action. Common sense flies out of the window. Officialdom runs riot. And businesses are hit with ludicrous requirements which may even close them down. Yet, the very reason why it is so hard to argue with this 'play safe' monster is that as soon as such modern shibboleths as 'hygiene', 'safety' or 'the environment' are invoked, then it seems that any regulatory action can be justified however irrelevant to the problem'.

Many people blame Brussels, which does bear much of the blame, but we must also hold our own Civil Service responsible. Mr Robin Teverson a Member of the European Parliament put it this way in a letter to the *Sunday Telegraph* on 8 October 1995: '... our own officials seem to delight in making good Euro-regulations bad. Every year farmers are required to fill in an IACS (Integrated Administration and Control System) form to get their grants. In most countries the resulting forms total 12-17 pages. In the UK the paperwork stretches to 87 pages. Many farmers reported that this form took nearly 50 hours to complete. Any attempt to hack back the red tape must start with Whitehall's dense thickets.'

RESPONSES TO REGULATION

I would now like to summarise the 'standard responses' of businesses and organisations when affected by the 'regulatory urge', and comment on what they mean when they call for change.

Large food businesses

This sector tends to repeat endlessly the same call for 'effective and sensible regulation', in order to ensure consumer confidence, safety protection and fair competition. These aims seem harmless but they are also self-contradictory. If 'big business' encourages over-regulation, claiming to protect consumers, it knows in reality that the extra costs may close smaller competitors by forcing up their overheads. This is not fair competition and it acts against the public interest by enabling variety to be reduced and food prices to be increased. The large businesses are furthermore in a strong position to take the line that public safety comes first, regardless of cost.

Local authorities

These bodies have a vested interest in more regulation in order to build bigger and more complex empires at taxpayers' expense and become more 'essential' to the public. They can use the 'safety' and 'public comes first' arguments to advance their cause, but in reality they mean that their interests come first. They are not concerned that there are no derogations for small businesses and prefer to lose them in favour of large businesses that are easier to police.

Government

The approach at Government level is that it must be seen to be concerned, and to be taking action, frequently by commissioning academic research; and if nothing significant appears to be happening it claims that its hands are tied by Brussels.

Universities

The response from this quarter is usually that funding has been cut or research grants are needed. They do not seek the easy solutions such as better hygiene practices or failures of enforcement, but tend towards more regulation and licensing leading to more stress on businesses and greater likelihood of food-poisoning outbreaks.

Small businesses
This sector believes in effective safety standards, but there are economic limits and only so many production hours in a day. In the recent *E. coli* case in Lanarkshire, possibly caused by just one hygiene mistake in one shop and an Environmental Health Officer (EHO) who missed it, the proposed solution of more regulation and licensing whilst well-intentioned, did not work in the *Salmonella* or BSE incidents and seems unlikely to achieve anything in the *E. coli* case. The imposition of more regulation destroys confidence and if nothing better can be devised, the system is likely to continue on a downward path. There are no derogations for small businesses on the argument that less stringent standards would put public health at risk and the costs of compliance therefore fall disproportionately on very small firms. The FSB position is that the basis of regulation should be simplified and requirements to demonstrate compliance should be appropriate for the size and type of business.

SOLUTIONS
The search for the way forward seems to have centred on the establishment of a new food standards/food safety agency. The small-business sector does not support the idea of another quango and 'talking shop' - it is surely better to examine the existing systems, slim them down, and ensure that they are working properly. We do, however, need to ask why persistent pressure for more regulation always fails - every time we tighten the rules, the incidence of food poisoning rises. I suggest that it is for one of two reasons, either:

(a)   our system of controls works so well that our natural resistance to infection is breaking down. In this case, we need a reduction in regulation so that some natural infection remains, sufficient to maintain our natural resistance. This, plus a return to teaching everyone, EHOs included, basic cleanliness and hygiene, proper cooking, food separation etc as taught in the '60s, should suffice to control the nastier bugs. So, our best course is a return to the old pre-Food Safety Act framework. Increasing Euro-directives are a problem but exchange visits with other European EHOs and inspectors could provide new insights. Or -

(b)   our system of controls works so badly because the complexities are such that neither businesses, the Health and Safety Executive (HSE) nor EHOs fully comprehend it. Also, if the rules are not kept simple or constantly need interpreting, then production time that should be wealth-creating, is clearly being wasted. Again the answer is to return to the regulatory framework of the '60s, when statistics show we were so much healthier and food poisoning cases were few.

REGULATION CONTROL

I would now like to turn to brief commentaries on aspects of regulation control of particular interest and concern to the FSB.

Brussels

Around 3000 Committees now produce Euro-Directives, and we believe the United Kingdom (UK) business community needs to be kept better informed. We need early notification (monthly) to all interested parties of:

- forthcoming rules, directives and issues for discussion at each meeting of the appropriate European committees;
- contact addresses of UK representatives on these committees;
- regular agendas and reports of the committee deliberations.

In the past, businesses often heard of Euro-Directives after they had been enacted, which made it too late for them to be changed. Input is therefore needed earlier to avoid expensive mistakes. We are, however, pleased to note that a start has been made by the publication in January of a news sheet by EUROPMI (European Small Business Organisation), reporting Committee meetings in Brussels and their subject matter. We would like to see the appropriate Government Departments assisting in the distribution of these news sheets to all businesses and adding to them where necessary.

Westminster

New regulations to be applied just in the UK and not simultaneously applicable in other European Union (EU) countries, are now risky and can cause trade distortion. Licensing, for example, as proposed by Professor Pennington (see The Pennington Group, 1997) to cope with the *E. coli* problem, may be subject to legal challenge. By imposing different restrictions on UK traders inapplicable to their EU counterparts, we are now at risk of discriminating unfairly against them in intra-EU trade. This may contravene the Competition Rules (Articles 85-94) of the Treaty of Rome, if not also Single European Market laws. We need a simple system with overriding powers to review, cancel or amend rules and directives that become outdated.

Scientific advances

These now occur rapidly, often making UK and EU rules obsolete before completion. For example, nitrate levels, enforced by the Nitrate and Surface Water Directives, were recently found by Aberdeen Medical School and others to be a risk to human health and digestion below levels now being set as maxima. Already millions of pounds have been spent on the obsolete 50 mg/l standard by Water Authorities, yet the rules remain in place. We would therefore recommend the setting up of a review body in consultation with the

European Commission (EC) and would suggest the involvement of EUROPMI.

LACOTS and HSE

Our members report confusion between LACOTS (Local Authorities Co-ordinating Body on Food and Trading Standards) and HSE about which regulatory fields are covered by which body. This needs resolving. There is also some friction in that the training and experience of HSE staff are generally regarded as superior to those of EHOs, which can lead to conflicting advice. There is therefore room for action to ensure consistency and also to ensure that businesses know the clear sectoral divisions.

Cabinet Office Deregulation Unit

This four-year-old unit has been useful but we are disappointed by its slow progress against the much faster rate of new legislation coming out. During 1996 the Department of Trade and Industry (DTI) revoked 93 regulations but introduced 224 new ones in the same period. We would like to see a faster deregulation flow rate, a more robust approach to Brussels, a stronger restraining influence by Brussels, and transfers of staff from regulating to deregulating work to achieve these changes.

Enforcement

We deplore the use of this term which encourages a confrontational approach to business. We prefer a more cooperative spirit with the provision of advice and guidance rather than just punitive action. Fines should be minimal except in serious cases, and be used only as a means of last resort. However, bearing in mind that this has not been very successful recently in providing balanced protection for business, we recommend that any new national food agency that may be set up should act as arbiter in pre-trial disputes.

Abattoirs

One thing that has become clear is that the recent £50 per hour inspection fee that abattoirs are now required to impose is a major cause of the loss of so many of our smaller abattoirs. Perhaps our firmest conclusion is that this charge must be rescinded. The fast throughput of large abattoirs now presents a greater risk of *E. coli* cross-contamination and quicker spread in the community, before containment, so we must encourage a trend back to smaller abattoirs, particularly in rural areas where the loss of small units has increased travelling distances, made prices uncompetitive and severely affected the viability of farms. Recent events have also shown how the larger abattoirs are now using their stronger bargaining power to force up Government payments for the BSE slaughter policy.

RECOMMENDATIONS
A summary of the main recommendations proposed in the interests of
the small food business sector is as follows:

- **improved communication**
  early circulation to businesses at the first stage of discussion, of
  EC health and safety proposals, preferably by EUROPMI monthly
  news sheets;

- **improved UK committee representation**
  ensure that the UK is represented on all EU Committees and that
  the UK food industry is kept informed at all stages of
  development;

- **scientific advances**
  set up effective machinery and procedures for quick review and
  amendment of Euro-Directives where this is justified by new
  scientific advances or safety measures;

- **HSE, LACOTS and EHOs**
  review policies and procedures with more emphasis on simple
  hygiene practices and less on enforcing the letter of the law;
  establish firm HSE/EHO functions so that business fully
  understands the areas for which each organisation has
  responsibility; equalise staff training and experience up to HSE
  standards

- **Deregulation Unit**
  step-up the Deregulation Unit work rate considerably with
  encouragement of restraint by Brussels;
  transfers of staff from regulating to deregulating work in Brussels
  and Whitehall;

- **derogations for small business**
  a one-man business should be the basic criterion for setting
  standards adjusted upwards for larger businesses. This would
  ensure that standards are set that can be easily met by the basic
  one-man business unit.

CONCLUSIONS
So, to conclude, let us 'keep it simple'. Let us worry about clean cloths,
clean work surfaces, proper cooking, etc. If we ensure that EHOs and
inspectors share these priorities, we can keep ourselves out of the
office and in productive work. It must be better to keep industry
working under simple rules that we all understand, rather than
destroying forests to create ever more waste paper.

And may I finally quote a passage taken from the Judgement on the *Listeria* case of Clydesdale Council *v.* Errington, which the FSB warmly applauds, as follows: 'The spirit of a number of publications and guidance, including the Report of the Joint Food & Agriculture Organisation/World Health Organisation Expert Consultation (Production No 7/1) in March 1995 concerning food hygiene inspections, while not an exact parallel, seems to encourage a sensitive, flexible and instructive approach by a Food Authority to enforcement. In a subject area such as this - where Provisional Microbiological Guidelines are stated to serve as no more than a starting point from which other investigations, including epidemiological evidence, can proceed, and where so much has still to be learned in respect of a fast-developing and changing subject - a dogmatic and unduly rigid 'policing' approach and philosophy by a Food Authority seems out of place, out of date and less than helpful. While certainty may make examination, control and enforcement easier, it must be obvious that it is not always possible in such matters. Accordingly, not only is great care needed, but detailed enquiry and fact finding are needed before critical steps are taken.'

REFERENCE

The Pennington Group (1997) *Report on the circumstances leading to the 1996 outbreak of infection with* E. coli *0157 in Central Scotland. The implications for food safety and the lessons to be learned.* London: The Stationery Office.

Marshall BJ & Miller FA (Eds)(1997) *Management of regulation in the food chain - balancing costs, benefits and effects.*
CAS Paper 36. Reading: Centre for Agricultural Strategy.

8 The impact of regulations on consumers and the food chain industries

Spencer Henson

INTRODUCTION

The policy environment within which the government regulates food safety is currently in a state of flux. On the one hand there is a seemingly never-ending demand for regulation of the food system to protect public health as a result, at least in part, of contemporary 'food scares'. On the other, there are concerns about the burden imposed on the food system by what is perceived, by some, to be overly onerous food safety regulation. Reflecting attempts to solve this dichotomy, there has been increasing interest in the efficiency of food safety regulation (see for example Breyer, 1993; Antle, 1995), which in turn has changed the thrust of the debate from regulation *per se* to 'good' regulation (see for example DTI, 1994).

Whilst there is agreement on the need to regulate food safety as a general principle, there is less agreement on when regulation is necessary, the forms regulation should take and, in particular, what is 'good' regulation. Although the notion that regulation should be 'effective', 'fair' and 'publicly acceptable' (HM Treasury, 1996) is not contentious, there is debate over how general principles such as these are actually defined and measured. Thus, whilst both the food industry and consumer groups would surely agree that a regulation which imposes heavy costs on food businesses but fails to protect consumers is ineffective and even unfair, there may be less agreement in cases where there is a direct trade-off between costs to food businesses and the level of food safety. Moreover in practice it may be very difficult to objectively assess whether a particular regulation satisfies these general principles and therefore is 'good' rather than 'bad'.

This paper attempts to throw some light on the current food safety regulation debate in the United Kingdom (UK) by addressing the following basic questions which tend to underlie differences in opinion over the need for, and effectiveness of, regulation aimed at ensuring the safety of our food supply:

- What are we trying to achieve with food safety regulation?
- What are the costs and benefits of food safety regulation?
- What forms might food safety regulation take?
- How do we assess the success or failure of food safety regulation?

These questions are discussed in turn below.

AIMS OF FOOD SAFETY REGULATION

Given that absolute safety (zero risk) is a scientific impossibility, contemporary discussion of food safety is framed in terms of 'acceptable risk', a concept which acknowledges that humans can only manage the hazards to which they are exposed and attempt to reduce risks to levels which are tolerable (see for example Fischoff *et al*, 1981; Douglas, 1985; Pidgeon *et al*, 1992). In this context, the objective of food safety regulation is not to make food **safe**, but to reduce the level of risk associated with food to some level which is regarded as more acceptable than that which would otherwise prevail. That is to make food **more safe**.

The economic literature on food safety further develops the notion of acceptable risk (Smallwood & Blaycock, 1991; Henson & Traill, 1993). Economists suggest that even if it were scientifically possible to reduce the risks associated with a particular food to zero (absolute safety), it may not be desirable to do so. Given that reductions in risk involve the use of resources, trade-offs have to be made between reducing food-borne risks and reducing other risks to human health (such as motor vehicle accidents or nuclear radiation) and between reducing food-borne risks and other social objectives (for example education or national defence). This suggests that there is some socially optimal level of risk associated with food (which is non-zero) which balances the full costs and benefits to society of higher levels of safety.

The model of food safety regulation presented above posits the rationale for food safety in terms of three questions: what is the prevailing level of risk?; what level of risk is acceptable?; and, in cases where the prevailing level of risk is unacceptable, how can the acceptable level of risk be achieved?

The established approach to the first question is based on scientific risk assessment whereby risk is estimated as the product of the severity of the health effects associated with a hazard and the probability that these negative consequences will be realised (see for example Anand, 1993; Henson & Traill, 1993; Adams, 1995). Whilst this model may at first sight seem an entirely rational approach within which to handle risk, it has been widely criticised by, amongst others, Brunk et al, 1991; Adams, 1995; Thompson, 1996; Millstone, 1996). For example, the framework depends on the availability of reliable estimates of the probabilities associated with particular hazards based on expert opinion. However, it is well documented that experts rarely agree with one another; scientists who appear to be as 'expert' as one another routinely produce quite different responses to the same question (eg Henson, 1997). One consequence of this according to Ulrich Beck (1992) in his book *Risk society*, is that individuals select from the range of experts available to them and thus may disagree with one another simply because they have chosen different experts.

Whilst there are established methods to assess prevailing levels of risks associated with food, there are no such methods to determine the level of risk which is acceptable. The literature on risk acceptability spans the social sciences, encompassing psychology (eg Fischoff et al, 1981), economics (Henson & Traill, 1993) and sociology (eg Douglas, 1992; Kasperson, 1992), and even the liberal arts in the form of philosophy (eg Douglas, 1985; Thompson, 1997). Whilst there is growing recognition that risk acceptability is defined not only in terms of scientific estimates of probability but also encompasses qualitative aspects, for example the degree to which a risk is perceived as voluntary or to be known by science (see Pigeon et al, 1992 for a brief review), there have been few attempts to incorporate such considerations into the policy process in an explicit and structured manner. There have been attempts by some government agencies to consider wider aspects of risk acceptability in regulation decision-making, for example the Health and Safety Executive. Such qualitative aspects of risk emphasise the degree to which risk acceptability is a function of the social, cultural and economic system within which we live - what is judged to be unacceptable in the UK today may be simultaneously judged acceptable in India, and maybe even as close to home as France.

Within any one country, the nature and level of risk associated with food which is deemed acceptable change over time. In part this is a function of scientific discovery which provides new and better means of reducing the risks associated with food. Simultaneously scientific discovery identifies 'new' risks to human health of which society was happily unaware. Unfortunately, the rate at which 'new' risks are discovered tends to outstrip the rate at which the means to control 'existing' risks are developed. Changes in risk acceptability also result from processes of economic and social change. As incomes have increased, and whilst better means to control risks have been introduced, the tolerability of even small risks has declined. Simultaneously, there has been a recognition that we are routinely subject to a wide range of risks and that these risks are not/cannot be adequately managed by the traditional institutions in which we previously endowed trust (Beck, 1992).

The complexity of the notion of acceptable risk necessarily means that judgments regarding the desirability of prevailing levels of risk are made by the political process whereby conflicting interests are competed off against one another. In recent times this process has been subject to close scrutiny following a number of food scares which have been interpreted by some as indicators that the food system, and the regulatory system which acts as a constraint on its activities, are failing. Thus, there have been calls for the existing regulatory system to be revised in an attempt to overcome perceived inequalities in the prevailing balance of interests through, for example, the creation of an 'independent' food agency (Lang et al, 1996; NCC, 1996).

Given that the prevailing level of risk associated with food is judged to be unacceptable, the next question is why is this so? The demand for government regulation to reduce the level of risk associated with food implicitly assumes that the market is failing; the normal operation of the market, given existing regulatory controls, is supplying a level of food safety which is considered inadequate. There is thus a case for government intervention to force the market to behave in such a manner that produces the desired level of food safety through restrictions on the activities of food suppliers and/or consumers. There are many reasons why markets might fail to produce the socially optimum level of food safety. Consequently, it is important to fully understand how the market is failing in any particular circumstance, in order to implement regulatory controls which address the problem at hand effectively. Some of the important potential market failures are outlined below.

Imperfect information
For consumers to evaluate effectively the significance of individual food-borne risk factors and assess the risk posed by each food product, information has to be available on the consequence of consumption prior to purchase. Whilst it must be acknowledged that consumers are imperfect problem solvers who collect limited information upon which to base their choices, it is evident that the information set available to consumers is itself imperfect. There are three basic problems in the provision of information on food safety by the market: the nature of food-borne risks themselves; the 'public good' nature of information; and asymmetries in the supply of safety information (which are related to market structure).

The nature of food-borne risks

Three broad categories of characteristic can be defined through which consumers discover the nature of food: search characteristics, for which information can be obtained from external sources through search prior to consumption (eg, price, colour, etc); experience characteristics, for which information on the nature of the characteristics is available upon consumption (for example taste, texture, acute food risk factors); and credence characteristics, for which information is only available some time after consumption (eg, chronic food risk factors).

All food-borne risk factors fall clearly into the experience and credence categories. Salmonellosis and other such food poisonings are experience characteristics which become obvious after consumption. Longer-term risk factors such as nutritional imbalance in the diet, food additives or pesticide residues are credence characteristics and consumers cannot judge their effects immediately upon consumption. In fact, many of the direct effects may never be apparent, and those that are observable may be confined to the longer term. In these situations consumers rely upon external risk indicators to indicate the level of food safety. These are product attributes which are known to be highly correlated with the level of experience or credence characteristics. Mitchell (1992) analysed consumer perceived risk towards a number of food products and the risk indicators employed in consumer choice processes. Important indicators identified were brand, product information, price, the nature of food packaging, and the nature of the food store and its ability to handle produce. The use of these product attributes as risk indicators underlines the need for clear legislation to control their misuse, for example labelling laws.

The provision of information can itself be seen as resulting from market allocation of resources to the production of information. This is explicitly seen in the purchase of food magazines which advise consumers in their choices, but is also implicit in the decision by consumers to use information provided in food markets, for example on labels. In the first case, the monetary cost to consumers is the purchase price of the magazine, book, etc. In the second case, it is the additional price of the food item to cover the cost of information provision. In both cases it costs the consumer time and effort to assimilate and assess the information.

The 'public good' nature of information

Directly information is published it yields benefits to society as a whole in addition to the private benefits accruing to the individual who pays for it. These social benefits, which result from the 'public good' characteristics of information, are not adequately taken into account in the marketplace, and as a consequence the market for food safety information is likely to be undersupplied.

The asymmetric nature of information

It is inevitable that food manufacturers and retailers are better informed about the nature of the products they sell than individual consumers. This asymmetry in the level of information possessed by buyers and sellers is important for the nature of the supply and demand for food safety in the market. In competitive market systems it is likely that sellers will divulge a great deal of this information in the marketing of their food products and asymmetries will be lowered. However, where suppliers possess a degree of market power the asymmetries will be maintained.

Within markets characterised by asymmetry of information, the more knowledgeable group, in this case food manufacturers, may be tempted to encourage consumer misperceptions about the safety of their food products. The seminal work on the implications of informational asymmetries is provided by Akerlof (1970). Consider a market with two food products, one relatively safe, the other relatively risky. Sellers of the products can tell which products are safe and which are dangerous, but consumers cannot. Therefore, although the safer product costs more to produce, it can only be sold in the market at the same price as the riskier product. As a consequence, food manufacturers only supply the risky product and the safer product is forced from the market.

An alternative scenario is possible. Safety issues are a major part of the marketing strategies of food manufacturers and retailers. In order to emphasise the benefits of their products, food producers may overstate particular risks in competing products. For example, manufacturers of low and reduced sugar products may overemphasise the risks of sugar consumption. Consumers' misperceptions of risk are reinforced and they are encouraged to buy safer foods than they would optimally choose. The result could be that the market supplies an excess of food safety.

Finally, food safety is used as a component of companies' product differentiation strategies. This can raise entry barriers, eg through the need for higher levels of research and development and advertising, and thus lead to greater levels of concentration in manufacturing and retailing, giving still greater information asymmetries, and perhaps higher prices.

Externalities and the social costs of food-borne risk

Consumer demand for food safety is driven by private costs and benefits with little consideration for the social consequences of changes in the level of food-borne risks: ill-health which results from food-borne risk factors imposes significant costs upon society which are externalities to private decisions about the acceptable level of food safety. These externalities include the cost of lost production, medical care, ill-health to other members of society, and surveillance and inspection. Therefore when consumers demand a higher level of food safety they yield external benefits to society as a whole, the value of which is not reflected in the market price. Thus food safety encompasses significant public good properties and, as is typical with public goods, the level of food safety supplied by the market is unlikely to reach the social optimum.

Distributional issues
The distribution of the benefits of increases in food safety between different socioeconomic groups within society is a particularly sensitive issue. The provision of food safety by the marketplace is driven by the ability and willingness-to-pay of private individuals. Consequently, the market will tend to direct lower-risk foods towards higher-income consumers and higher-risk foods to lower-income consumers. The acceptability of higher risks being borne by the lower socioeconomic groups in society obviously raises ethical questions (Douglas, 1985).

Even though it may be demonstrated that food markets are failing, due to one or a combination of the reasons outlined above, and that the level of risk associated with food exceeds what is considered acceptable as a result, this may not be a sufficient rationale for government intervention. On pure efficiency grounds, government regulation should only be pursued if it can be clearly demonstrated that the safety of food will increase as a direct result (and would not have occurred anyway), and that the value placed on this improvement in safety exceeds the costs involved. However, in practice quantifying the costs and benefits of food safety regulation is very difficult and invariably relies on a series of assumptions which, at best, are subject to challenge. (The UK Government now requires the costs and benefits of all new regulatory proposals to be assessed, including quantification where possible. Further details of this process of Regulatory Appraisal are given in Cabinet Office, 1996.)

COSTS AND BENEFITS OF FOOD SAFETY REGULATION
The regulation debate which has transcended much of the developed world in recent years has focused attention on the costs and benefits associated with all forms of government intervention. Further, in many countries, for example the United States, UK and Canada, an explicit attempt to evaluate these costs and benefits forms part of the policy process when proposals for new regulations are being considered (OECD, 1996).

The key costs and benefits associated with food safety regulations are discussed below. In many ways the distinction between costs and benefits is an arbitrary one; effects of a regulation which are evaluated negatively are costs, and effects that are evaluated positively are benefits. In certain cases what are regarded as costs by one economic interest group are regarded as benefits by another.

Benefits to consumers and society
The aim of food safety standards is to reduce the risk of food-borne disease below the level which would otherwise prevail. Thus the benefit to consumers is a reduction in the risk of ill-health and/or loss of life due to food-borne disease and, in turn, the costs associated with ill-health or loss of life which are avoided. The range of effects includes:

- Loss of income due to time unable to work;
- Psychological costs of pain, suffering and apprehension associated with ill-health and loss of life;
- Costs of medical care;

Sometimes these costs are borne by consumers themselves and in others by society as a whole. For example, in the UK the costs of medical care are borne collectively by tax payers rather than by the individual requiring treatment. Sometimes the benefits associated with reductions in the risk of food-borne illness may be offset by certain costs which are imposed on consumers by food safety regulations. These can include higher food prices and a reduction in the available choice of food products. There is evidence that consumers may place a great emphasis on such costs relative to what are perceived to be relatively small reductions in the risk of food-borne disease.

Costs to government
The key costs for government of food safety regulations are summarised in Figure 1. In most cases the responsibilities for implementation and monitoring/enforcement will fall upon different agencies within government. For example in the UK, food safety regulations are made by and reflect the policies of the National Government but are enforced by Local Authorities or specialist agencies. Further, the magnitude of the costs for government will depend on the nature of the rule-making process. For example, the greater the level of consultation with interested parties as part of the formal regulatory process, the greater the costs of implementation. (This is an example of where the Government might choose to expend greater resources itself in an attempt to minimise the costs on other economic agents, for example the food industry.)

Figure 1
Costs for government of food safety regulations

Activity	Costs
The legislative process	Drafting regulation
	Consultation
	Regulatory impact analysis
	Legal costs
Monitoring/Enforcement	Inspection/Investigation
	Testing
	Record keeping
	Prosecution

Source: Henson (1997)

To a certain extent the costs for government of regulating the food system depend on how suppliers respond to the regulation. For example, if the rate of non-compliance is high, then enforcement agencies will need to expend greater resources in an attempt to enforce regulations. This will tend to occur when the costs of compliance for food suppliers is high, suggesting a trade-off between enforcement costs for government and compliance costs for suppliers. However, it is possible for enforcement costs to be high even if enforcement has little impact on the behaviour of suppliers, for example if enforcement agencies lack information on the degree to which firms already comply or the appropriate action to induce compliance.

Costs to business
The category of costs associated with food safety regulations which has probably received most attention is the compliance costs imposed on business. Compliance costs are defined as the additional costs necessarily incurred by businesses in meeting the requirements laid upon them in complying with a given regulation. There are two key elements to this definition. Firstly, it covers the costs which are 'additional' to those which would have been incurred in the absence of the regulation. Secondly, it refers to those costs which are 'necessarily' incurred when complying with the regulation.

Although the range of costs associated with compliance will depend on the specific characteristics of the regulation, it is possible to devise a list which covers the major factors involved (Figure 2). In part these costs are associated with actually achieving compliance with the regulation, such as through capital investment or staff training, and in part to demonstrate compliance through record keeping.

Figure 2
Costs of compliance with food regulation

Cost incurring activities	
Administration	
Analytical services	
Capital investment:	Buildings
	Equipment
Distribution	
Input prices	
Inspection	
Labelling	
Maintenance	
Packaging	
Quality control/assurance	
Staff:	Additional
	Employee time
	Management time
Training	

Source: Henson (1997)

Of particular concern is the impact of regulations on small firms since there tend to be significant economies of scale associated with costs of compliance. Consequently, the government may deliberately apply different regulatory or enforcement standards to smaller firms in an attempt to offset the proportionately higher compliance costs. This is termed 'regulatory tiering'.

The foregoing discussion demonstrates the wide-ranging economic impact of food safety regulations. Not only do restrictions on the free operation of the market result in both costs and benefits, in many cases these costs and benefits accrue to different economic interest groups, leading to potentially significant distributional effects. Consequently, the government must look to ways of achieving the desired level of food safety which impose the minimum costs on the economic system as a whole, and on vulnerable groups (for example low income consumers and small- and medium-sized food businesses) in particular. As will be clear from the next section the economic effects of food safety regulation relate not only to the degree to which the government intervenes, but also the instruments it employs in doing so.

FORMS OF FOOD SAFETY REGULATION

Regulation of food safety can take a number of forms (Figure 3) which differ in the degree to which they impede freedom of activity (Ogus, 1994). At one extreme, information measures require suppliers to disclose certain facts about their products, but do not otherwise restrict behaviour. At the other, suppliers may require prior approval of a product from an official agency before being permitted to release it onto the market; such approval will be based on pre-specified safety criteria.

Figure 3
Forms of government food safety regulation

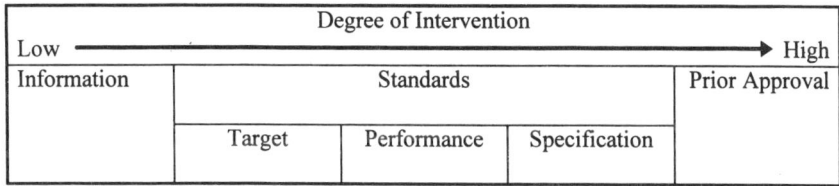

Degree of Intervention				
Low ⟶ High				
Information	Standards			Prior Approval
	Target	Performance	Specification	

Source: Henson (1997)

Food safety standards allow suppliers to release products onto the market without any prior control, but suppliers which fail to meet certain minimum safety standards commit an offence. Food safety standards can take three main forms. Target standards do not prescribe any specific safety standards for the supplier's products or the processes by which they are produced, but impose criminal liability for pre-specified harmful consequences which arise from their products. Performance standards require certain levels of safety to be achieved when the product is supplied, but leave suppliers free to choose the mechanisms through which they meet such conditions. Specification standards are applied both to products (product standards) and the processes by which those products are made (process standards) and can take positive or negative forms, either making the use of particular ingredients or particular production methods compulsory, or prohibiting the use of particular ingredients or production methods.

In the case of food safety, government regulation normally takes the form of standards which generally correct market failures, in particular information deficiencies and externalities, more effectively than redress through private law and information disclosure requirements.

Private law is generally not regarded as an effective mechanism for regulating food. The courts are generally only able to act retrospectively to compensate an individual who has suffered harm, whilst access to redress through private law is dependent on the availability of the resources required to do so.

Similarly, the efficacy of mandatory disclosure of information, eg, in the form of food safety warnings, is generally regarded as limited in the case of food safety. Such mechanisms depend on the ability of consumers to process food safety information in an appropriate manner and to take action to avoid food-borne hazards. Consequently, information tends to discriminate against consumers with poor educational attainment. Further, information disclosure only influences the actions of those who have direct contact with a hazard rather than those affected as an externality to the action of others. (A particularly interesting case of the use of information disclosure is Proposition 65 in California which requires that consumers are warned if they are likely to be exposed to a substance added to food which is carcinogenic. The rationale behind this action is that consumers can take private litigation action if they are injured by consumption of a food and were not prior warned.)

As a general principle, it is desirable to maximise the freedom of suppliers to choose the manner in which they meet the specified regulatory objectives. This will enable suppliers to minimise compliance costs by implementing the most efficient method of complying with the specified regulatory standards and promoting innovation in compliance technology. However, this general principle may be offset by greater costs for other economic groups which are party to the regulation. For example, standards which permit considerable freedom in the method of compliance are generally more difficult to monitor and enforce and consequently impose greater costs on enforcement authorities. In addition, there is a tendency for suppliers to over comply when given discretion regarding the method of compliance in a bid to offset uncertainties over what is deemed sufficient to satisfy the regulatory standard.

From a cost-effectiveness perspective, target standards which render it illegal to supply food which is deemed to be unsafe appear a desirable approach to food safety regulation. The specified goal of the regulation can be translated directly into prohibited outcomes and it is then left to suppliers to implement appropriate mechanisms to ensure these prohibited outcomes do not occur. This permits firms to implement the method of compliance which is most efficient given their own particular cost structure.

However, target standards can also impose significant information costs on both enforcement agencies and suppliers which, in certain cases, may outweigh such efficiency gains. For many food-borne risks the relationship between human ill-health and exposure to a particular hazard is separated by space and/or time. Consequently, the costs to enforcement agencies in determining a causal link between the actions of a particular supplier and the exposure of consumers to a hazard are often very high. In this situation all but the most obvious violations of the standard may remain unchallenged since enforcement agencies constrained by budgetary considerations will be reluctant to pursue any action unless there is a high probability of success in the courts.

In the case of target standards it is the responsibility of individual suppliers to determine the quality of their own performance which will ensure compliance with the standard. This can impose high information costs on suppliers associated with uncertainty over which practices are or are not acceptable under the standard. Consequently, there may be an inherent tendency for firms to implement procedures in excess of those required to comply, as security against violation of the standard. An example of such an approach is the UK Food Safety Act 1990 which makes it an offence to sell for consumption food products which are unfit for human consumption.

The costs of implementing performance standards are greater than for target standards since the regulator has to predetermine the quality of performance by suppliers which is acceptable given the goals of the regulation. However in many cases, such as where firms in the market or the products they produce are relatively homogeneous, there will be economies of scale associated with this task being undertaken by one central agency rather than individual suppliers. Furthermore, determining when a violation of the standard has occurred is generally easier and less costly since performance standards are more closely defined and compliance can be directly monitored at the place of production. Thus enforcement costs are generally lower.

Since performance standards define the actions of firms which are permissible more precisely than target standards, there is less flexibility for firms to determine the most efficient method of compliance and consequently compliance costs tend to be higher. However, since the actions required of firms are more precisely defined, there is less uncertainty associated with performance standards. Therefore, information costs tend to be lower and there is less tendency for firms to over-comply.

Specification standards are more precisely defined than either target or performance standards, laying down a comprehensive series of rules about the nature of food products and/or the processes by which they are produced which, it is assumed, will ensure the desired level of food safety. Consequently, at any point in time there is less uncertainty associated with specification standards, both for enforcement agencies in terms of determining which products or processes comply with the standard, and for suppliers in terms of what has to be done to achieve compliance. However, as a result of their precise nature, specification standards tend to become obsolete as technology develops and may need to be regularly updated. The nature of the regulatory processs is such that the momentum with which standards are updated will tend to lag behind the rate of technological change. Consequently, standards will tend to arrest innovation, resulting in significant losses of social welfare.

The precise nature of specification standards implies high implementation costs for regulatory agencies since even relatively straightforward food safety targets need to be translated into detailed input and/or production parameters. However, once implemented, specification standards are relatively easy to enforce since the enforcement agency has simply to verify in the case of a positive standard that the prescribed input or process has been used or, in the case of a negative standard, that the prohibited input or process has not been used.

Whilst the detailed nature of specification standards minimises the information costs to firms of determining how to comply, there is little flexibility for firms to adapt the method of compliance to their particular cost structure. Further, unlike target or performance standards, there is little incentive for firms to develop compliance technologies which reduce compliance costs. However, since there is little discretion over how to comply with the standard there is less uncertainty regarding the costs of compliance. Further, there is likely to be less variation in compliance costs between individual firms in the market.

In conclusion, food safety regulations can potentially impose high costs of compliance on food businesses which in certain cases feed through as higher prices to consumers and inhibit innovation. Consequently, it is important for policy makers to adopt regulatory forms which achieve the desired level of food safety at the minimum cost to food suppliers. In most cases this implies maximising the flexibility afforded to suppliers to achieve the desired level of food safety in a manner which is most appropriate to their own particular circumstances, even if this in turn imposes greater costs of enforcement on local government or other responsible agencies.

ASSESSING THE SUCCESS OR FAILURE OF FOOD SAFETY REGULATION

Given that food markets are already highly regulated, it is implicit in demands for further food safety regulation that existing government controls are failing to provide the desired level of safety. Experience suggests that there is never a shortage of interest groups which consider current government policy is failing, indeed government failure appears to have become ubiquitous to modern society (Bovens & Thart, 1996). However, for the purposes of a more constructive contribution to the food safety regulation debate it is necessary to examine what separates success from failure a little more closely. Three issues, salient to the current discussion are discussed below.

Inevitability of failure

Would we have had Bovine Spongiform Encephalopathy (BSE) if the UK government had not altered the existing regulatory controls on processing temperatures for animal feed in the 1980s? Would the fatal outbreak of *Escherichia coli* in Scotland at the end of 1996 have occurred if we had had registration rather than licensing of food premises? Maybe, but maybe not! It is only when we start wondering about what might have been, that we fully realise that what *has* happened need *not* have happened. This inevitably leads us to question why existing regulations, which were supposed to protect the safety of our food supply, failed.

It is very easy to look back at the decisions that were made in the past and fall into the 'wisdom after the event trap' whereby our estimates of the outcome of historical decisions are strongly influenced by what we know actually happened (Bovens & Thart, 1996). Once we know the outcome, the events that occurred seem very logical, more predictable and maybe even inevitable; we seem to 'just know it would happen'. Of course what we are doing is underestimating the complexity of the problem and the general uncertainty faced by government when the regulation was actually promulgated and performing an ex-post reconstruction framed in terms of what we know today. We are always wiser after the event and therefore on this basis will automatically judge much of the existing controls to have failed.

Relativity of failure

Because of the lack of a fixed benchmark which applies regardless of time and place and is universally agreed by all with an interest in food safety regulation, it is virtually inevitable that a particular regulation will be deemed a failure by someone. Below are a few examples by way of illustration:

- The benchmark against which food safety regulations are assessed tends to change over time and there is a tendency to evaluate regulations against what is possible today rather than what was possible when the regulation was actually promulgated, for example, as science provides better means to control existing food-borne hazards or identifies new hazards in food of which we were previously unaware.

- Individual interest groups adopt their own benchmarks against which to assess the success or failure of food safety regulations. In many cases these benchmarks may not accord with those adopted by government when the regulation was originally promulgated.
- In many cases there may be no formal benchmark against which to assess food safety regulation, either because the objectives of the regulation were not formally specified when it was originally formulated or because the specification of such a benchmark is not possible. In this case there is no way to formally judge whether a regulation is a success or failure.
- Even in cases where a bench mark does exist, there is no consensus on how much deviation from the intended outcome represents a failure. If the intended reduction in the incidence of food poisoning was 30% but it actually only declined by 25%, is this a failure? What about if it had only declined by 20%? Would a decline by 35% have been an outstanding success?

Imperfect markets *versus* imperfect regulation

The food safety regulation debate, like all forms of government policy, involves a trade-off between imperfect markets and imperfect regulation (see for example Wolf, 1990). Not only do markets fail to achieve the outcome that society demands but so, in many cases, do regulations. Regulation is a very blunt tool which is relatively easy to promulgate but incredibly difficult to implement and enforce in such a way that firms comply in the manner intended. Further, should a regulation fail, it can in certain circumstances be very difficult and time-consuming to remove.

Having decided that existing regulatory measures have failed to achieve the desired level of food safety is not sufficient grounds to proceed to new regulatory controls, it is also necessary to understand why existing controls have failed. This requires an understanding of the process by which regulations are made and then implemented (Figure 4). Thus there needs to be a recognition that the government is not the only party involved in the regulatory process: we must also consider the actions of enforcement officials and food businesses which comply, or do not comply, with existing regulations. For example, the regulation may not have had the desired effect because a significant proportion of food businesses failed to comply or food businesses complied in a manner which was not anticipated. Alternatively, the regulation may have been misinterpreted, and therefore misenforced, by enforcement officials. In all cases, before it is deemed that a regulation has failed, it is necessary to examine why the regulation had the effects it did. Maybe it was not the regulation at all, but simply the manner in which it was implemented, and that small changes to the regulatory process, for example through revisions to enforcement guidelines, would have produced the desired outcome?

Figure 4
Regulatory process

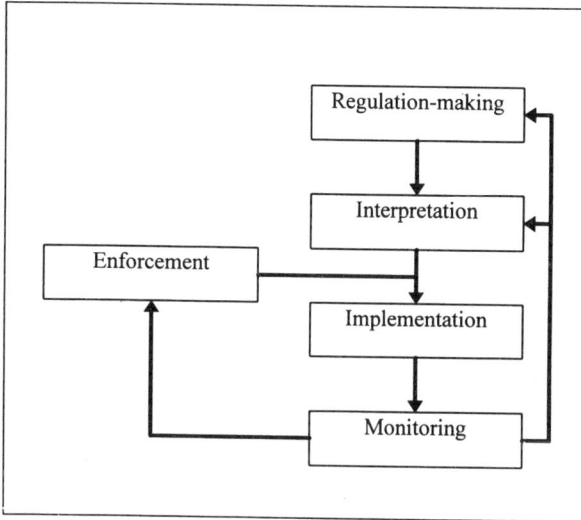

Source: Henson (1997)

CONCLUSIONS
This paper has not provided any answers, but has served to illustrate the great complexity of the issues raised by the food safety regulation debate. It is hoped that it will serve, at least in part, to overcome the tendency of certain interest groups to over-simplify the impact of regulatory controls on food markets, both in terms of the wider costs and benefits and how judgments are made about success or failure. It is only through a full understanding of these issues that effective regulatory controls can be implemented which balance the full effects on consumers, the food industry and the government and achieve a level of food safety which meets the needs of society.

REFERENCES
Adams, J (1995) *Risk*. London: UCL Press.
Akerlof, G A (1970) The market for lemons: quality, uncertainty and the market mechanism. *Quarterly Journal of Economics* **84**, 488-500.
Anand, P (1993) *Foundations of rational choice under risk*. Oxford: Clarendon Press.
Antle, J M (1995) *Choice and efficiency in food safety policy*. Washington: AEI Press.

Beck, U (1992) *Risk society: towards a new modernity*. London: Sage Publications.

Bovens, M & Thart, P (1996) *Understanding policy fiascoes*. New Brunswick, USA: Transaction Publishers.

Breyer, S (1993) *Breaking the vicious circle: toward effective risk regulation*. Cambridge: Harvard University Press.

Brunk, C, Haworth, L & Lee, B (1991) *Value assumptions in risk assessment*. Waterloo: Wilfrid University Press.

Deregulation Unit, Cabinet Office (1996) *Regulation in the balance – a guide to regulatory appraisal incorporating risk assessment*. London: HMSO.

Douglas, M (1985) *Risk acceptability according to the social sciences*. London: Routledge & Kegan Paul.

Douglas, M (1992) *Risk and blame. Essays in cultural theory*. London: Routledge.

DTI (1994) *Thinking about regulating*. London: Department of Trade and Industry.

Fischoff, B, Lichtenstein, S, Slovic, P, Derby, S L & Keeney, R L (1981) *Acceptable risk*. Cambridge: Cambridge University Press.

Henson, S J (1997) Estimating the incidence of food-borne *Salmonella* and the effectiveness of alternative control measures using the Delphi Method. *International Journal of Food Microbiology*, **35**, 195-204.

Henson, S J & Traill, W B (1993) The demand for food safety: markets imperfections and the role of Government. *Food Policy* **18** (2) 152-162.

HM Treasury (1996) *The setting of safety standards*. London: HM Treasury.

Kasperson, R E (1992) The social amplification of risk: progress in developing an integrative framework. In: Krimsky, S & Golding, D (Eds) *Social theories of risk*. Westport, Virginia: Praeger.

Lang, T, Millstone, E, Raven, H & Rayner, M (1996) *Modernising UK food policy: the case for reforming the Ministry of Agriculture, Fisheries and Food*. London: Thames Valley University.

Millstone, E (1996) Food safety: the ethical dimension. In: Mepham, B (Ed) *Food ethics*. London: Routledge.

Mitchell, V-W (1992) *Consumer choice of risky food products: the role of indicators in food choice*. Paper presented at the conference 'Consumers and Food-Borne Risks : An Interdisciplinary Workshop', The University of Reading, May 1992. [unpublished].

NCC (1996) *National Consumer Council Bulletin August 1996*. London: National Consumer Council.

OECD (1996) *An overview of regulatory impact analysis in OECD countries*. PUMA/REG(96)7. Paris: OECD.

Ogus, A I (1994) *Regulation. Legal forms and economic theory*. Oxford: Clarendon Press.

Pidgeon, N, Hood, C, Jones, D, Turner, B & Gibson, R (1992) Risk perception. In: Royal Society. *Risk: analysis, perception and management.* London: The Royal Society.

Royal Society (1992) *Risk: analysis, perception and management.* London: The Royal Society.

Smallwood, D M & Blaylock, J R (1991) Consumer demand for food and food safety: models and applications. In: Caswell, JA (Ed) *Economics of food safety.* New York: Elsevier.

Thompson, P (1996) Competing conceptions of risk. *Risk, Health, Safety and Environment*, **12**, 361-380.

Thompson, P (1997) *Ethics and food safety.* Paper presented at the conference Social Construction of Safe Food, Trondheim, April 1997. [In press]

Wolf, C (1990) *Markets or governments: choosing between imperfect alternatives.* Cambridge: MIT Press.

DISCUSSION

Mrs Joanna Wheatley (Farmer) said that her main concern about regulation and controls relates to the possible transference of genetic material and whether adequate systems are in place for post-licensing surveillance, and monitoring of the effects of the use of biotechnologies. The problems she envisaged were herbicide resistance and the risk of 'super weeds' and a possible build-up of antibiotic resistance in cattle.

Dr Geraldine Schofield said in reply that the herbicide resistance issue has been addressed by the Advisory Committee on Releases to the Environment (ACRE) on which she has served as a member. One of the questions debated early on was based on the 'precautionary principle' of 'what if x and y happen?', and debate has now moved on to 'if it does happen what is the increased risk of harm?' She agreed with the questionner that there will be a certain amount of gene flow in terms of some of the crop plants now on the market and agreed also that in order to avoid resistances in pest populations or multiple herbicide resistances, there has to be integrated crop management; but as herbicides are not sprayed onto a natural population, the risk of harm by gene transfer to the natural environment is pretty small. A problem that could arise is the re-emergence of a weed into a major crop species. These questions are however being asked and are matters for the manufacturers of the herbicide and the crop producers. With regard to antibiotic resistance build-up, the risks were addressed by the Advisory Committee on Novel Foods and Processes (ACNFP) which concluded that there was a potential, although extremely small, risk of the transfer of the antibiotic resistance marker in the animal gut.

Dr Schofield said that if we are to realise the advantage of the technology, the question of monitoring has to be addressed partly by the industry that is providing that technology, and partly by those responsible for the public funding.

Ms Sheila McKecknie felt that one of the problems of regulatory systems is that they often specify procedures to be applied in isolated situations or to specific products, rather than addressing the more global or more general problems of which antibiotic resistance is one. She therefore asked whether there is any evidence of regulatory frameworks that can deal with the generality as opposed to the specific product outcome?

Dr Geraldine Schofield accepted the importance of this broader approach to regulation and added that academic researchers in the USA are addressing this very issue but no conclusions are yet available.

Mr David Gaunt (British Simmental Cattle Society) referred to the intense pressures on the beef industry which appeared almost to amount to a requirement that it should produce food in a sterile environment. This, of course, would be impractical and his proposition was that as we have a very diverse population with different cultures and different standards of food preparation and hygienic understanding, the consumers' organisations should press for consumer education and for the reintroduction within our school curriculum of those factors which will help to bring common-sense back into food hygiene.

Ms Sheila McKechnie accepted that consumer education provides an important part of the solution to reducing the level of food poisoning, certainly in the field of microbiological safety. She also expressed the view that we should stop seeing the BSE problem as a debate between the farmers and the consumers since polarisation does not in these complex issues, help to take the debate forward. Consumers and industry do have a number of things in common but they do also face a number of issues where their interests are diametrically opposed; it is the clarity of those issues in terms of the detail, that make for a good regulatory process.

Marshall BJ & Miller FA (Eds)(1997) *Management of regulation in the food chain - balancing costs, benefits and effects.*
CAS Paper 36. Reading: Centre for Agricultural Strategy.

9 Regulatory impact analysis and cost assessment of proposed United Kingdom and European Community legislation

Lucy Neville-Rolfe

INTRODUCTION

Thank you for volunteering me for the challenging after-lunch slot. I will aim to keep my contribution punchy and picturesque. I am the Director of the Deregulation Unit which aims to minimise regulatory burdens on business and others, and so contribute to the work of the Office of Public Service. The Deregulation Unit reports to the Chancellor of the Duchy of Lancaster. We also report quarterly to the Prime Minister, and advise the Deputy Prime Minister as necessary. However, I should start by emphasising that the deregulation initiative, which I coordinate across Whitehall, is not just about sweeping away outdated rules and regulations. It is also about simpler paperwork and consistent enforcement in administering regulations. It is about striking the right balance between cost and benefit when making new regulations, whether domestic or European. My speech will describe the regulatory appraisal system we have introduced to help lawmakers to achieve this.

All this can and is being achieved without compromising any protection necessary to safeguard the public. I challenge anyone to cite even one example where necessary protection has been jeopardised by deregulatory changes we have made.

OUR APPROACH

It is encouraging that during this morning's session, there was good support for goal-based, proportionate and non-prescriptive regulations. These are key principles of the deregulation initiative.

Our programme also aims to unharness innovation, promote the competitiveness of United Kingdom (UK) business, and remove market barriers. This generates jobs, increases consumer choice, and reduces prices for consumers. We attach particular importance to close consultation with business and others, and getting that process embedded right across the government machine. This is why we have set up a Deregulation Task Force of representatives from business and why we have held a series of seminars across the country on key areas, including food and drink. We also go out to speak at and listen at conferences such as this one today. We have also set up a network of Local Business Partnerships, in which some of this afternoon's speakers are involved. One hundred Local Business Partnerships to improve the dialogue between local business and regulators in local government have now been set up across the country. This is an important way of encouraging openness and consultation.

Another important strand is better communication. We try to promote plain English, less paperwork, and a tolerance of simplicity in Government, in the enforcement community, and indeed in business itself. As Sheila McKechnie, Chief Executive of the Consumers' Association, said this morning, what is needed is clear, understandable regulation. Simple things will be understood, particularly by small business. Lots of red tape will not.

EXAMPLES OF SUCCESSES

Let us look at one or two examples of recent successes that illustrate the impact that the initiative has had. Who would have imagined five years ago that we would be happily shopping on Sunday, shopping until late at night, and taking our children to pubs (at least in some areas)? Who would have thought we would make progress in very difficult areas like the threshold for Value Added Tax and statutory audit? The latter will rise from £90 000 to £350 000 shortly. And who would have thought that food legislation could be simplified at all? I am sure previous speakers will have mentioned the work that has been done on labelling and additives regulations to bring the requirements together and make them less confusing - without loss of protection. I am also pleased to report that we hit our target of 1000 repeals and amendments by the end of 1996.

REGULATORY APPRAISAL

The main purpose of Regulatory Appraisal is to enable Ministers to balance out various factors and take a considered view of the relative costs and benefits of proposed regulation. The process is set out in a booklet called *Regulation in the balance - a guide to regulatory appraisal incorporating risk assessment* which we published in 1996 with fuller guidance on Compliance Cost Assessment in a companion volume *Checking the cost of regulation*. These documents are also available on the Internet on the Cabinet Office Deregulation Unit home page under http://www.open.gov.uk/co/du/duhome.htm. I want to emphasise the key points that Government Departments are now asked to address when thinking about regulating. These are:

- Ask **'What is the purpose of the proposed regulation?'** A lot of the time, people get stuck right here. Departments must be absolutely clear about the reasons why they are proposing change.

- **Consider what sectors the regulation will affect, and how.** For example, if you are proposing changes to the law on discos, assess the impact on neighbouring residents and property as well as on business and their lively customers.

- **Identify the problem and the harm.** What is the risk that the harm will occur?

- **Consider alternative approaches.** There is always the option of **doing nothing,** or improving enforcement of existing rules. This is sometimes difficult, but it can be the right answer. Potential regulators should also look at voluntary measures, such as codes of practice or advertising. Sometimes, these will be the most effective way forward. In other cases new regulation will be needed.

- **Identify the impact of all the options on the risk**

- Where new regulation is identified as the best option, **make the regulations goal-based** to avoid unnecessary prescription.

- **Consult everyone who has an interest.** Do not send a 200-page document with a short deadline and wonder why no-one replies. Prepare a document based on good principles of communication - simple, based on the right points and not too long.

- **Undertake a 'small business litmus test'.** Regulators must talk to two or three representative small firms about how they would manage the proposed changes. This information is then incorporated into the structured assessment and informs Ministers' decisions.

- **Take account of political and equity considerations.** The process does not rule out political factors. Our analysis is designed to reflect real life, including the need to take account of the perceptions of various groups and the general public as a whole, and of equity and distributional effects. Environmental and consumer effects can also be brought out in this part of the analysis. What we ask Departments to do is to articulate the political ramifications of the proposals clearly for Ministers, not to adjust the basic figures on cost or risk.

- **Take the total benefits, and the total and typical costs, and compare the two**. This should give you a measure of proportionality and a feel for the impact on a typical operation.
- The final step in the process known as **'signing in blood'**. This is where the responsible Minister certifies that he or she has read the cost and risk assessments and is satisfied that the draft regulation strikes the right balance between cost and benefit.

EXAMPLES OF USE OF ASSESSMENT
A couple of recent examples illustrate the benefits of this system - the proposed Fire Precautions (Workplace) Regulations implementing European Community (EC) rules on fire safety and the Producer Responsibility (Packaging Waste) Regulations recently made by the Secretary of State for the Environment. In both cases decisions on how to regulate were fully informed by Compliance Cost Assessment, and were influenced as a result of the exercise. The Guarantees Directive under discussion in Brussels is an example of an area where useful progress has been made as a result of cost assessment work done in the UK. Indeed the EC have now agreed to carry out such an assessment themselves.

Ministers who make new regulations which affect business, charities or voluntary organisations report to the Deputy Prime Minister monthly on the number of new regulations being made so that the balance of costs and benefits can be monitored centrally. This monthly Ministerial regulatory monitoring system has been in place for nearly a year now and is providing vital new information to enable us to do our job better.

BUSINESS-FRIENDLY ENFORCEMENT
The enforcement of regulations is just as important as the regulations themselves. You may have heard of the 'Green Card' principles of business-friendly enforcement. These include rights to written notification of what action is needed and why, and a chance to make representations unless immediate action is needed. This allows disputes to be resolved at an early stage and gives greater scope for firms to comply in a way which makes good business sense. The Green Card principles are ones we think all good enforcers follow, but they are being brought in across the statute book to ensure a greater consistency of approach.

These new business rights came in last year for health and safety legislation. Their operation has already been reviewed, and the review has shown that business likes the Green Card and that these new rights do not jeopardise necessary protection. This is not surprising, because both enforcers and business benefit from efforts to help people understand and comply with the law. Everyone wins if you are open about risk and uncertainty and if you explain to people why they must take action. Then people will usually comply - as compliance theories and experience with my own children suggest!

BETTER FORMS AND SURVEYS
It is important to improve forms and surveys, so that they are brief, to the point, and impose as light a burden as possible. We are also looking ahead to the next century and loading regulatory data onto the Internet and other Information Technology vehicles. By the end of this year, we will have 600 items of guidance and forms on our Internet gateway. This will ensure that the general public has easy access to simple information on legal requirements such as those relating to fire, health and safety, and tax.

BETTER EUROPEAN REGULATION
The request to talk about Europe was very appropriate because in the last year, the Deregulation Unit has changed its focus. It is now devoting significant resources to establishing good regulatory principles at the European Union (EU) level. 'Getting it right the first time' in Europe is even more important than doing so nationally because there are fourteen other Member States to persuade if a change is needed. The first promising sign was the language used by Jacques Santer when he was appointed EC President in 1995. He announced that he was going to have 'less but better' regulation. This chimes with our own theme 'fewer, better, simpler'

Last year the EC issued regulatory policy guidelines for all EU Government officials. These guidelines emphasise the importance of assessment, consultation, clarity and simplicity. The Dutch Presidency are very interested in deregulation. They are among the pioneers of good regulatory policy and have organised a Government symposium in The Hague to look at impact assessment and improving regulation at EU level.

The Internal Market Council is well known to the food sector experts because of its role in decisions on food law. In the last year, small teams known as 'SLIMS' (Simpler Legislation for the Internal Market) (CEC, 1996) from Government and business across the EU have started rolling reviews to look at specific areas of Single Market legislation, such as Intrastat. They are considering how well the legislation is working, and whether it can be simplified. I believe there is good prospect of simplification, particularly during the UK Presidency next year. We are already working up our UK Presidency agenda with the Commission and the Austrians, who will hold the Presidency after us.

We have also introduced a check-list on the implementation of European law. A big issue for Government is that in the past we have sometimes taken what issued from Brussels, and then 'gold-plated' it by adding extra requirements or details. The result has been more burdens on business. My vision for implementing European law is the opposite. We should consider whether the existing domestic regime can be simplified when the new Directive is brought in, as was done for trade marks. The result should then be better for business, not worse.

CONCLUSION
Three key points emerge from this analysis.

● First, structured analysis of the costs and benefits is now a requirement for new law that affects business, charities or voluntary organisations. In time, this should improve the quality of new regulations.

● Second, think small. Consultation on the likely practical impact of a new law is key. The analysis of the effect on small firms is especially important. They suffer most from having to divert crucial entrepreneurial resources into coping with the cumulative impact of regulations.

● Third, keep things simple. We want Government and the EU to think simply but clearly. We want rules communicated in a way that people understand. We want enforcers to communicate simply and clearly so that people understand the law with which they must comply. Finally, we want business itself to think simply, and not to be the source of requests for complex and confusing prescription.

REFERENCES
CEC (1996) *Simpler legislation for the internal market (SLIM): a pilot project.* COM(96) 204 final. Brussels: CEC.
Deregulation Unit, Cabinet Office (1996) *Checking the cost of regulation.* London: HMSO.
Deregulation Unit, Cabinet Office (1996) *Regulation in the balance - a guide to regulatory appraisal incorporating risk assessment.* London: HMSO.

DISCUSSION

Mrs Maeve Robertson (National Federation of Consumer Groups) expressed support for the deregulation process which she felt, in some cases, can bring benefits for consumers. She urged, however, the inclusion in the procedures of some appropriate mandatory arrangement under which consumers' interests, in the form of a 'consumer impact statement', could be taken into account in the costs assessment analyses undertaken in relation to proposed regulatory changes; an automatic process of reference and consultation with consumers' organisations would, she felt, provide ease of access to the machinery which would be generally helpful.

Ms Neville-Rolfe said in reply that consumers' interests are recognised as an important part of the regulatory assessment system and undertook to review the procedures with particular reference to the request for ease of access for consumers on equal terms with business and other interests.

Mr John Corbet-Milward (Wine and Spirit Association) asked the speaker to expand on the ways in which the Deregulation Unit (DU) seeks to influence other government departments.

Ms Lucy Neville-Rolfe explained that various methods are utilised depending on the circumstances, but the key point is that the DU must find effective ways of working closely with them all. The Cabinet Office is staffed in relation to the workload and consultations necessary within Whitehall and with all Government Departments - all Departments have at least one person working on deregulation, and others have their own Deregulation Units, including the Ministry of Agriculture, Fisheries and Food, whose team are represented at this conference. Also, within the constitutional structure of cabinet committees, there is the 'Committee on Competitiveness' that looks about once a quarter at deregulation issues submitted by the Cabinet Office Deregulation Unit and by individual Secretaries of State. Influence is also brought to bear on Departments through the 'feedback loops' - an arrangement under which the outcome of Deregulation Unit consultations with manufacturing businesses, enforcement authorities and other relevant interests are referred to the appropriate Departments in the interests of full and effective communication and understanding.

Marshall BJ & Miller FA (Eds)(1997) *Management of regulation in the food chain - balancing costs, benefits and effects.*
CAS Paper 36. Reading: Centre for Agricultural Strategy.

10 Development and drafting food legislation

Margaret Murray

INTRODUCTION

In his book *The future of law* (Susskind, 1996) Richard Susskind has pointed out that we live in 'hyperregulated times'. According to Mr Susskind 'we are all subject in our social and working lives, to a body of legal rules and principles which is so vast, diverse and complicated that no-one can understand their full applicability and impact..... Being hyperregulated means that there is too much law for us to manage'. This experience of hyperregulation is felt in many fields of law from housing to taxation to food law. It is neither confined to food law nor to the United Kingdom (UK).

FOOD LEGISLATION IN THE UK

An essential plank of the analysis of the legal system applicable to food law which was reviewed in the 1993 report of the Food, Drink and Agriculture Task Force entitled *Proposals for deregulation* was that UK legislation is very detailed in comparison to legislation produced in other European countries. I would argue that detail is not a feature applicable to UK law only nor is it only a feature of the implementation of EC Directives. In this paper, I will examine why we have detailed regulations in the food area and whether anything can be done to alleviate the position.

It is a fact that since the 19th Century, legislation in the UK has become more detailed. The Sale of Goods Act 1893 was about 20 pages long, whereas the modern law of sale of goods fits into two sections of a loose-leaf encyclopedia. Why is this? In my opinion it is the result of the policy-makers' wish to add more certainty to the general principles of legislation as set out in the law relating to the sale of goods, including food. No longer is it sufficient to rule that food must be fit for its purpose and conform to the descriptions issued about it, but more specific examples must be set out, explained and covered within the scope of the statutory provisions to give more certainty without the need to go to court for interpretation.

The policy-makers' wish to avoid the necessity for court-made law is one aspect of the increase in legislation applicable to consumer products. Another is the development of European legislation and the need to combine the wishes of the policy makers from various Member States into one document. As has been pointed out in the Task Force review, legislation at the European level is often drafted with intentional ambiguity in order to reach a satisfactory policy conclusion to which all can agree because all have the opportunity to interpret the ambiguity according to their requirements and wishes.

OTHER EUROPEAN COUNTRIES
Looking at the amount of law in other countries it is useful to consider perhaps German food law. According to the information I have received, German food law covers about 4000 food law texts which amount to about 20 000 pages of legal statements. In fact I have received a paper from a German lawyer who has compared the loose-leaf text of German food law to the loose-leaf text of the French publication (Dehove, 1996) and the English publication *Practical food law manual* (Rowell, 1988). He points out that these two publications comprise two loose-leaf files only, whereas his German law comprises 37 thick files. He also refers to the EU *Official Journal* which can be measured in metres of text. My colleague, Dr Feldmann of Cologne has repeatedly tried to support the simplification of German food law by publishing essays and comments on judgements but he feels this has not met with success. In Germany the law is complicated by the existence of both national government and regional states government with their own food law in each case. There are also different judicial decisions on the same facts in different regions.

In considering the complexity of food law it is necessary to bear in mind that food law is very much an applied law. One is taking pure legal principles and applying them to everyday materials and everyday functions. It is therefore not surprising that policy makers have sought to ensure that their policy is set out in detailed regulations to avoid doubt in interpretation and enforcement. However, this admirable objective is not achieved in all cases at all times in all places. This is a state of imperfection which, to some extent, has to be accepted.

FOOD, DRINK AND AGRICULTURE TASK FORCE RECOMMENDATIONS (1993)

Looking at the specific recommendations of the Task Force, I would like to make the following comments.

Liquor licensing and policy implications

The Task Force commented on the licensing requirements affecting UK grocery retailers. I would like to set that against the contribution to profit which the sale of intoxicating liquors makes for UK grocery retailers and the importance of safeguarding the public and particularly minors from alcohol abuse and unregulated access to intoxicating liquor. We have a fairly free regime in the UK as far as access to alcohol is concerned, but this could be lost if alcohol abuse is not dealt with through the system of local licensing which has worked very well in the UK. I would therefore point out that this is not simply a matter of cost but also of public policy.

Approach to enforcement

Do we have a culture which is more concerned with obeying the letter of the law than achieving it's objectives? There is no doubt that this is manifested from time to time in enforcement attitudes. It has to be remembered that regulatory law is a discretionary law in that not every regulatory offence can possibly be prosecuted. The prosecution therefore has a discretion as to which cases it chooses to prosecute. In my recent experience I find that enforcement authorities may tend to prosecute small businesses which do not have significant resources for their defence because in such a case of transgression a conviction can be obtained easily against unrepresented defendants although no damage has been incurred or even any prospect of risk complained of.

In certain cases of regulatory transgression the UK system of issuing a caution instead of prosecuting is more appropriate. I have however found that a 'Catch 22' situation can arise in such cases. I recently advised a large catering company in relation to a prosecution for a mouldy sandwich. This company exercised their right not to submit to an interview where what they said could have been used in evidence against them. The alleged offence was not part of any pattern and it appeared to me that to have cautioned the company would have been the most appropriate route. I was however told by the enforcement authorities that they would have issued a caution except for the fact that the company had not agreed to an official interview.

In another case I acted for a small trader who was accused of selling jewellery which resembled food. No one had seen any risk in the production of these stones which were wrapped in brightly coloured cellophane. To some extent they did not differ from products sold as candles wrapped up in cellophane and presented as lollies which are sold by a major national retail firm. These clients cooperated in every way with the enforcement authorities and agreed to an interview under caution during which they admitted that the product breached the Food Imitation Regulations of which they had previously been unaware. They asked for advice on how to conform with these Regulations but received none. They were prosecuted and then came to me for advice. They had no choice but to plead guilty but were discharged by the magistrates. Again, I thought that this was a case where a caution should have been administered, but I was told by the Prosecution that, despite the cooperation of the clients in the interview with enforcement authorities, it was intended to proceed because an offence had been committed and an admission had been made.

Implementation of Deregulation (Model Appeal) Order 1996

It appears to me that in these cases the best means forward is through the Deregulation (Model Appeals) Order 1996 which will allow clients to appeal against summonses in such cases where more appropriate enforcement action is available. I believe the Model Appeals procedure is a step in the right direction and flows from the deregulation initiative. I do not know if it is intended to implement it in respect of UK food safety in the near future but it would be helpful if an announcement could be made. I do not know what the Opposition view on this is and again, it would be useful to have a policy statement on this point. The important point to note is that it is not necessary to prosecute to enforce regulations. Regulations can be enforced through caution and resort to prosecution in the case of serious persistent offenders.

Drafting of European food legislation

Legislation now originates in the food area mainly in Europe. There are strong criticisms on all fronts of the way in which European legislation is drafted and formulated. Ambiguities are often left in on purpose by the legislators. In other cases particular interest groups have a desire to see a specific set of words used. Sometimes this is for legitimate reasons, but sometimes it is also a matter of ego, commercial advantage or national pride which gets in the way of the real purpose of the legislation.

As a lawyer I would comment on the specific general recommendations of the Task Force as follows:

- *Risk assessment*
  I agree that legislation should be based on a genuine assessment of risk and should be proportionate to the problem;

- *Cooperation and consultation*
  This is an important aspect. I believe that the Government does make reasonable efforts to consult but often European time-frames do not leave sufficient time for this activity. It is to be hoped that this can be resolved at the European level;

- *Compliance cost analysis*
  Again I would support this but it does require the cooperation of industry and the working together by lawyers and their clients to properly assess the cost of compliance;

- *Consolidation and simplification*
  It is a desirable objective to adopt clear and simple language. However, it is often in the areas where technical input is required that the language becomes most convoluted and complicated. The food hygiene area is one which has been held in this respect and I would submit that it is not a question of lawyers' language but sometimes of the language required and recommended by technical advisors;

- *Pilot schemes*
  I am not entirely sure what is meant by pilot schemes and how they would work;

- *Scrutiny and review of regulations*
  I would agree with these objectives although I think they may be time consuming;

- *Litmus test*
  The Small Firm's Litmus Test appears to be a good idea and lawyers in the field are in a good position to feed back their clients' problems in these areas.

- *Language used*
  It is recommended by the Task Force that the language used should be that of the main user of the food law who they define as the small businessman, employees, pensioners and ordinary citizens. In a sense this is correct as long as the language used is 'middle-of-the-road'. However, legislation drafted in pure 'Scouse' would not be clear to the majority of the Law Lords even though it would be intelligible to a 'Scouser';

Clarity, simplicity and brevity should be the object of the draftsman in legislation, but where certainty is required in every conceivable situation, brevity and simplicity may suffer. I would agree with the scrutiny of legislation to eliminate unnecessary and complicated details in Bills. Citizens should be informed of the intention of the legislation. Lawyers and solicitors can look at the intentions of the policy makers and the Courts recognise that it is legitimate to consult the records of the debates in Parliament to a form of conclusion as to the intention of the legislators.

Notes on statutes

Notes on statutes are helpful. However they should not usurp the role of the Courts because this would place too much power in the hands of non-accountable administrators. The position of the Courts as supreme in the interpretation of law should not be diluted. As lawyers we often see differences arising between guidelines issued and the statutes themselves and in some cases, clients find themselves in a position of not knowing whether they should comply with the guidelines, or with the statute.

CONCLUSION

The main recommendation I would make is that improvement in legislation must take place at the European level because all significant UK food law will now stem from that source. Without understandable legislation at European level, courts cannot interpret food law properly. The European Court of Justice itself has had trouble in interpreting some of the legislation coming from Europe. I have heard Judges comment that they can try to interpret law but if there is no meaning behind the law to interpret then they find it impossible to draft decisions that will make sense. The result however is that in some cases the European Court of Justice has to make law in default of any sensible way of interpreting the text provided through the European legislative system.

The task ahead of the European Union (EU) is to improve the drafting of legislation, to insist on proper scrutiny by lawyers before it is finalised and no doubt to tackle the real problems faced with a multiplicity of working languages and official language texts of legislation. The EU has already begun to tackle the problem of clear drafting of legislation. In a Council's Decision of June 1993 on the quality of drafting of Community legislation, the EC published guidelines for the making of Community legislation. These guidelines state that the words of any statutory provision should be clear, simple, concise and unambiguous.

The European Parliament passed a Regulation in July 1994 calling for transparency of Community Law and its codification. Lawyers and experts involved in food law have for many years pointed out the unnecessary complexity of the legislation and the different approaches to different products and issues which result in uneven regulation in the food area. This is partly due to the structure of the Community Institutions and partly to political issues in the EU. It is perhaps an unavoidable aspect of the initial development of the EU and we can hope to look forward to a period of consolidation, clarification and deregulation which I can assure you will be welcomed by lawyers as well as their clients.

REFERENCES

Dehove, R A (1996) *Réglementation des produits, qualité, répression des fraudes*. Paris: Lamy.

Food Drink and Agriculture Task Force (1993). *Proposals for deregulation*. Deposited in the House of Commons Library. [unpublished]

Rowell, R A (1988) (Ed) *Practical food law manual*. London: Sweet & Maxwell.

Susskind, R (1996) *The future of law*. Oxford: University Press.

Marshall BJ & Miller FA (Eds)(1997) *Management of regulation in the food chain - balancing costs, benefits and effects.*
CAS Paper 36. Reading: Centre for Agricultural Strategy.

11 Enforcement of food safety legislation

David Statham

INTRODUCTION

It is of great importance from the standpoint of the enforcer and the Enforcement Authority, that if food law is to achieve its objectives, the legislative measures must be acceptable and accepted by all. So, before embarking on a more detailed analysis of what the enforcer requires of legislation - that it must be suitable for the purpose, enforceable, fair, effective, necessary, and with a transparency of purpose - I would, by way of introduction, like to touch briefly on the need for a balanced approach with prosecution as very much the last resort.

My own local authority has set up a 'food forum' which brings the team of enforcement officers together with representatives of the food industry on a regular basis, to share information and exchange views on all aspects of food handling and preparation and the application of the complex range of food hygiene legislation. Every year we issue ten times more food safety awards than we do prosecutions; and I cannot recall a situation where a food business that has been given a caution has subsequently been prosecuted - a serious 'rap across the knuckles' delivered in an 'official' way has proved to be an effective method of dealing with most of our problem cases and ensuring that nothing further goes wrong. I would now like to develop the various criteria that in my view comprise the principles of good regulation that are acceptable to the food industry and capable of enforcement in the interests of the safety of the consumer.

SUITABLE FOR THE PURPOSE

It is important that legislation actually does the job for which it is intended. It is perfectly possible in framing legislation to intend to tackle one problem but, by dint of lack of consultation or bad drafting, to produce a final product that does not deliver what was intended. For example, the Food Safety Act 1990, a very laudable statute which brought food legislation up-to-date and which set out to provide a very good framework for safe food production, recognised the importance of the training of food handlers in ensuring safe food. Statistics point clearly to the fact that practically all food-borne disease arises out of ignorance, and I have never yet come across a food business that set out intentionally to poison its customers. However, when the training provision was finally incorporated into the General Food Hygiene Regulations the intent of the original Act had been changed: instead of requiring all food handlers to be 'trained', they were required to be 'trained, instructed or supervised' - a very different concept that does not fit the original purpose in the sense that it does not help to redress the problem of failures of businesses where staff had been instructed and supervised by other staff who were just as ignorant of safe food-handling techniques as those they were instructing. Examples of the problems of unsuitable legislation are the many cases of outbreaks of food-borne disease where the proprietor's reactions have been 'I did not realise I was doing anything wrong' or 'I have always done it that way'; but the second aspect is that not only have they done it the wrong way, but have passed on these malpractices whilst instructing others.

ENFORCEABLE
Legislation does sometimes need to be enforced, otherwise people drift into bad habits with dire consequences. Furthermore, the penalty for non-compliance has to be a sufficient deterrent to ensure that some people are brought into line. By way of illustration of legislation that is difficult to enforce, we have in Leicester a measure that requires the licensing of street traders, but the fines for non-compliance are so small that the vendors literally treat them as a business overhead - they accept that they are breaking the law, offer to pay their fines as quickly as possible, and then get on with repeating the breach. We have actually had to go to the extent of taking out injunctions to ensure that our enforcement time and effort is not wasted.

In the field of food safety there appears over the years to have grown up a confusion over what is a legal requirement and what is good practice. The regulations that have been drafted over the past few years in respect of temperature control are very much a case in point. The original temperature-control regulations had so many exemptions in relation to the time food could be handled and displayed at ambient temperature as to make enforcement impossible. It was once suggested that to get a conviction in respect of these regulations you would need to employ a private detective to keep food under surveillance at all times, or, better still, to install hidden cameras to record the amount of time the food spent at various temperatures. The regulations were therefore totally unenforceable. The new regulations are a little better but still have a significant number of loopholes. Suffice it to say, if what we require is to produce best-practice advice, then that is what should be done. But to draft legislation which is unenforceable is to waste everyone's time.

FAIR

Regulation and legislation need to be fair and it is essential that they are equitably applied, and repealed or amended when they become outdated. By way of illustration here, I would point towards the Shops Act (1950) which until recently controlled the opening of shops and the hours which could be worked by shop workers, and imposed restrictions on trading on Sundays. For many years it was an offence to sell fish and chips from a fish-and-chip shop on a Sunday, but perfectly all right to sell them from a 'Chinese Take-Away'; it was also illegal to sell a bible from a church book stall but all right to sell risqué magazines in a newsagents. These are just two of the examples of unfair legislation that was largely discredited. It is important that legislative provisions are fair and defensible if we are to ensure their effective application.

EFFECTIVE

When new legislation is introduced, how do we measure its effectiveness? The 'acid test' is whether or not it achieves what it set out to do. For example, did the introduction of the Dangerous Dogs Act prevent children getting bitten by dogs?

When the Food Safety Act (1990) provided powers for enforcement officers to serve Improvement Notices this appeared to be an excellent way of bringing premises up to standard without recourse to more draconian enforcement measures such as prosecution. My own authority has served many such notices - we have never had to resort to prosecution for non-compliance and we have seen dramatic improvements in food hygiene standards.

Some companies have, however, objected to receiving formal notices which has lead to the now infamous 'Minded To' procedure introduced in the Deregulation and Contracting Out Act (1994). In other words, authorities now have to serve a notice giving notice of their intention to serve another notice. My authority has calculated that if and when, as the Government have indicated, this provision is applied to all environmental-health legislation, it will, on the basis of current notice numbers, cost a further £40 000 per year to implement this deregulatory process with, one could argue, less effectiveness.

My team of enforcement officers operate under agreed procedures drawn up in accordance with ISO 9002 standards. These procedures include provision for officers to discuss with the proprietors of businesses the action they propose to take and the reasons for that action. They also listen to requests for extending timescales and also alternative solutions. Against that background, which is after all the procedure laid down in the appropriate enforcement code, the 'Minded To' procedure seems to be a somewhat ineffective burden on the ratepayer!

NECESSARY

It is also essential to ensure that proposed legislative controls are really necessary. Consultation with those responsible for enforcement and with the businesses likely to be affected is of paramount importance. What appears to happen, however, is that a worthwhile and necessary proposal can be brought forward, but by the time it has passed through the two-pronged machinery based in London and Brussels, it emerges in a form that is so radically changed as to make the new measure unnecessary. That was the fate of the Registration of Food Premises Regulations when what was needed was selective licensing linked perhaps with registration and prior approval. What the complex procedures eventually produced was registration which could not be refused and which was merely an information-gathering exercise. As many businesses thought this scheme to be an unnecessary bureaucratic exercise, the Government considered removing it or alternatively removing the provision to require a busines to register in advance of opening, which was in fact the only useful part of the exercise.

TRANSPARENCY OF PURPOSE

It is sometimes not entirely clear what is the purpose of some legislation - the statute appears to say one thing whilst the guidance, or lack of it, and vibes coming from Whitehall, say something else. It is essential for good legislation to be well drafted, clear, concise and to come complete with guidance as to its purpose and interpretation. By way of illustration I would point to the Specified Bovine Offals Order (which subsequently became Regulations) to tackle Bovine Spongiform Encephalopathy (BSE). The intention to bring in this Order was flagged up in summer 1989 and the Order was eventually introduced in November of that year. The Order was rushed out and Local Authorities who were then the enforcing bodies actually received their copies of the legislation several weeks after the Order came into force. This action taken in two stages created uncertainty - either the matter was important and hence the 'rush job', or it could not be that important since the enforcers were relying on their copy of *The Times* for the detail of the legislation. At the same time, Ministers were insisting that these measures were purely precautionary and that there was absolutely no risk of BSE being transmissible to humans.

The confusion was furthermore compounded by the Regulations requiring abattoirs to undertake complex surgical procedures without any guidance as to the approved method of doing this or indeed the implications in public-health terms of getting it slightly wrong. It was therefore no great surprise that there was not universal compliance with the Regulations either under the Local Authority regime or subsequently under the Meat Hygiene Service. No-one was ever given the slightest hint that leaving behind a tiny piece of spinal cord when the carcase was sawn in half could literally prove fatal!

SUMMARY

I have I hope, made a case for useful, well-drafted, enforceable legislation and emphasised in particular the importance of consulting with those responsible for enforcement, and also with the businesses to which regulations need to be acceptable and workable, about what regulatory measures are, or are not, required. It is to be hoped that the legislative changes which hopefully will flow from the Pennington Enquiry will fit this specification; perhaps a good test of the need for an 'independent' food-safety agency might be whether or not Professor Pennington's recommendations (see The Pennington Group, 1997) can be implemented without them being rendered ineffective. If they can, then we probably do not need a new agency; if they cannot, then we probably do.

REFERENCE
The Pennington Group (1997) *Report on the circumstances leading to the 1996 outbreak of infection with* E. coli *0157 in Central Scotland. The implications for food safety and the lessons to be learned.* London: The Stationery Office.

Marshall BJ & Miller FA (Eds)(1997) *Management of regulation in the food chain - balancing costs, benefits and effects.*
CAS Paper 36. Reading: Centre for Agricultural Strategy.

12 Enforcement of food standards legislation

Paul Allen

INTRODUCTION

The implementation and enforcement of food standards legislation is an important part of the responsibilities of local authorities. These bodies, working at the local level with food businesses, research institutes and consumers, also have much to contribute to the policies and to the formulation of the regulatory measures they have to operate. Local government has gone through a series of major reorganisations during recent years and so also have the local authority associations under a scheme that on 1 April 1997, brings together the Association of County Councils (ACC), the Association of District Councils (ADC) and the Association of Metropolitan Authorities (AMA) into one body to be called the Local Government Association (LGA). The main development in the context of this paper on food standards law and its enforcement, is the establishment of a Public Protection Committee (PPC) with a policy agenda of direct relevance to the subject matter of this conference. The key themes that will be addressed by the PPC are prescribed in its Policy Agenda as follows:

- close links between environmental health and wider *sustainable development*/environmental protection/Local Agenda 21 agendas;

- changing role of *regulation and enforcement* in public protection services and deregulation challenge:
  (i) issues of consistency of enforcement; reduction in 'red-tape'; and business-friendly approach
  (ii) Local Authorities Coordinating Body on Food and Trading Standards (LACOTS); 'one-stop shops'; home authority principle; development team approach

- powers: threat of further centralisation

- resources.

Against the background of these organisational changes and issues, it is helpful to have some appreciation of the myths and misunderstandings relating to assertions of over-zealous enforcement before turning to the question of deregulation (which should perhaps be more helpfully and constructively described as 'sensible legislation'), the European and United Kingdom (UK) dimensions of food law, and the approaches of the Government, the opposition political parties, the European Food Law Association of the United Kingdom (EFLA/UK) and the Institute of Trading Standards Associations (ITSA) to the future structure of food-law organisation and administration.

ENFORCEMENT MYTHS
In November 1994, LACOTS published its findings having investigated 74 published allegations of so-called unprofessional practices. Of the 74, twenty related to food control; seven to trading standards and sixteen to environmental health, a total of 43. Of these, five were found to have some substance. Some typical examples are as follows:

- Allegation that a particular District Authority informed a naval base that under food law it must discontinue the centuries-old tradition of stirring Christmas pudding with wooden oars.
  The named District Council does not exist and all environmental health authorities in the region deny ever considering, or offering, such advice.

- Allegation that a County Council took wrongful and excessive action in prosecuting for 20 unpriced items. Seventeen were allegedly marked. Fined £600.
  Authority claims action was result of proprietor(s) repeatedly ignoring oral and written warnings. Photographs show total absence of price information on the retail premises. Press Commission found the journalist should take greater care to ensure accuracy.

- Allegation that a London authority was blessed with commonsense in overruling another authority which had insisted on packages carrying lower case metric markings.
  Authority notes the compliment and records it only did what 99% of colleague authorities would have done.

- Plant nursery uses disused quarry on their land to deposit leaves and old compost. Alleged County Council said this was controlled waste and legal action would be considered to prevent dumping. Only when local MP was involved did Council retract and issue apology.

  Case involved County Council, District Council and National Rivers Authority who were concerned for the safety of the environment. Extensive dumping of compost, vegetable matter etc constitutes a danger to ground water due to contamination with leachate and risk of explosion due to landfill gas migration. Decision reversed following legal opinion that the waste could be classified as agricultural waste; therefore existing material need not be removed, nor continued dumping prohibited.

LOCAL BUSINESS PARTNERSHIPS

In order to deal with the changing role of regulation and enforcement, the need for consistency of enforcement and the reduction of 'red-tape' eg, the relaxation of the Sunday Trading laws, a constructive approach developed in East Sussex has been the launch since 1993 of seven Local Business Partnerships, one for each of the seven districts and boroughs in the county. A 'Next Steps Seminar' will shortly be organised to provide an opportunity for all the relevant agencies, ie, environmental health, trading standards and chambers of commerce, to meet and discuss how to make a reality of a 'One Stop Shop' concept for businesses *via* Business Link Sussex. (Business Links are promoted by the Government to provide help to businesses for training, investment, import/export problems etc.) Unfortunately, it is not possible for this forum to deal with resource problems such as the reduced budgets likely to be available when the present countywide East Sussex trading standards service is split into two parts under the forthcoming local government reorganisation.

EUROPEAN LEGISLATION

The European Community Inspection Service as set up under Directives 89/391/EEC and 93/99/EEC has had difficulty with resources, particularly staff, and so, to date, it has only visited/inspected twelve Member States. Inspections are planned for Austria, Spain and Portugal later this year. The Directive 89/391/EEC resulted in a Commission report to the European Parliament in 1994, describing how the service had been established and the Additional Measures Directive (93/99/EEC) required a report to Parliament in 1996 describing the implementation programme. It has not yet been published. Neither has the Green Paper on the future of food law in the community, but it is expected to be launched in The Hague next May.

The Temporary Committee of Inquiry into Bovine Spongiform Encephalopathy (BSE) set up by the European Parliament recommended in its draft report that the Community institutions should be strengthened; President Santer in commenting on the report to the European Parliament on 17 January 1997 indicated his wish for a new European Food Safety Agency.

UK FOOD LEGISLATION

Whilst the food industry and the enforcement authorities are concerned that action is needed to simplify and reduce the volume of food legislation and are cooperating in the deregulation initiative and in other relevant exercises, the series of food safety incidents and public anxieties have focused attention on the effectiveness of the organisational arrangements for the making, administration and enforcement of food law.

The Government has recently announced that to regain the confidence of consumers in the safety of food, they intend to set up a Food Safety Council, chaired by an independent Food Safety Adviser, to advise Ministers on matters relating to the safety, quality, labelling and authenticity of food. The Chairman of the Council will have a duty to communicate information relating to the work of the Food Safety Council to Parliament, the media and the general public.

For the Opposition parties, the Labour Party has made a clear commitment to setting up an independent food standards agency. The function of the agency will be consumer protection and its overriding priority will be the safety and quality of food; and the Liberal Democrat party proposes a completely independent authoritative stand-alone Food Commission, accountable to Parliament like the Audit Commission.

In a thoughtful, knowledgeable and constructive article in the *British Food Journal* in November 1996, Mr Charles Cockbill, the Chairman of EFLA/UK expressed the following personal views:

- the responsibility to make the necessary food safety law has to remain with Parliament and the Government

- the Government will always be concerned to ensure the economic health of the agriculture and food industries

- the present structure and content of UK food law is in order and does not need radical revision

- there have been complaints of over-enthusiastic enforcement but these have been no more than a few localised 'hotspots'

- cooperation and coordination of enforcement through LACOTS works effectively

- officials in the Ministry of Agriculture, Fisheries and Food (MAFF) and the Department of Health monitor developments, assisted by independent experts and report to Ministers

- most issues have to be decided on the balance of probabilities and it is therefore easy for decisions to be disagreed with

- the result is often confusion in the consumer's mind

- this seems to be the nub of the dissatisfaction with the present system

- it could therefore be sensible to invest in a separate food agency (separate that is from existing government departments) to undertake the monitoring and surveillance roles and the tendering of advice for action to Ministers.

The main functions of such an agency would thus be the ongoing assessment of scientific and medical developments, control of food surveillance programmes, responsibility for the expert committees, the commissioning of its own research, the submission of reports and advice to Ministers, and publication of those reports.

The Institute of Trading Standards would go further and incorporate food within a wider consumer affairs and consumer protection Government Department or Agency. That body would clearly have an input into food policy and would also ensure that all those involved in regulation were coordinated effectively. It should also be required to set down standards of enforcement and ensure the appropriate allocation of resources for the enforcement of consumer protection legislation. There should be a Cabinet Minister with a consumer affairs portfolio (as there was in 1974) and, as far as possible, regulatory responsibilities should be discharged at local level by local authorities which should have the resources to be able to do so.

CONCLUSION
Developments in the field of food safety are moving rapidly in the run-up to the General Election on 1 May 1997. The Government's acceptance of all the recommendations of the Pennington Report (Pennington Group, 1997) and the announcements of food policy proposals by the Opposition parties, mean that food safety issues will be a priority for any new Government.

REFERENCES

CEC (1989) 89/391/EEC Council Directive of 12 June 1989 on the introduction of measures to encourage improvements in the safety and health of workers at work. *Official Journal of the EC* L183.

CEC (1993) 93/99/EEC Council Directive of 29 October 1993 on the subject of additional measures concerning the official control of foodstuffs. *Official Journal of the EC* L290.

Cockbill, C (1996) An independent food agency? *British Food Journal* **98**(6) 5-7.

The Pennington Group (1997) *Report on the circumstances leading to the 1996 outbreak of infection with* E. coli *0157 in Central Scotland. The implications for food safety and the lessons to be learned.* London: The Stationery Office.

Marshall BJ & Miller FA (Eds)(1997) *Management of regulation in the food chain - balancing costs, benefits and effects.*
CAS Paper 36. Reading: Centre for Agricultural Strategy.

13 Food law administration and organisation - options for the future

Wyn Grant

'INDEPENDENCE' - WHAT DOES IT MEAN?

I want to start by injecting a note of scepticism into this whole debate. The first question I want to ask is about a word that recurs in this debate - 'independence'. Students of politics use the term 'hurrah words' to refer to words that give us a warm glow, that just have positive associations. 'Independence' is one of these words. One therefore has to be very careful about how it is used in a debate. No-one is against independence, but what does it mean?

Any new agency that is set up in the area of food safety cannot be completely independent. It is going to have to be publicly funded if it is going to do its job properly. This means it is going to have to be accountable to Ministers and through them to Parliament for the use of public funds. Some people might consider that it should be independent in terms of the expertise that it uses. It should, according to this view, draw more on experts that are not employed by, or have other links with, the food industry. Unfortunately, there are not many experts on food safety who do not have links with the industry. So any new agency is going to have to draw to some extent on the body of existing expertise. Perhaps what people really mean when they talk of independence is independent of the food industry - or at least perceived to be independent.

CONSUMER CONFIDENCE IN FOOD

It is important that we are clear about what is 'broke' and what has got to be fixed. If we do not know what our objectives are, we cannot

120

make useful recommendations about structure. Listening to this debate over the last few months, it is clear that the consensus view is that there is a need to restore consumer confidence in food after a series of food scares, notably that over Bovine Spongiform Encephalopathy (BSE) and the *Escherichia coli* outbreak in Scotland. A more radical view is that the present policy-making system is defective and does not provide consumers with adequate protection.

But is institutional change the solution to either objective? Political scientists are sceptical about institutional tinkering because they think that it is often a substitute for real change. Would a change in structure lead to different decisions? Would it provide different advice? These are key questions that have to be asked in relation to any institutional option. No structure is going to avoid a food scare, particularly if the media want to have a 'health scare of the week'. Moreover, the really important questions are ones of policy rather than structure - for example, what stance should be adopted on genetically-modified foods?

What I am going to do in the rest of my presentation is to review a series of options. The government has recently come forward with proposals which are not to be implemented until after the general election and I will say something about these later in my talk.

ORGANISATIONAL OPTIONS

Option 1. To abolish the Ministry and Agriculture, Fisheries and Food (MAFF) and redistribute its responsibilities elsewhere
Advocates of this view point out that there is no other industry that has its own Ministry and urge the need to sever the links between government and the relevant client groups. The Common Agricultural Policy accounts for half of the European Union (EU)'s budget and is a very complex policy. Hence, it needs a centre of specialist expertise headed by a Minister of Cabinet rank to handle negotiations. All other EU Member States have agriculture Ministers: the Prodi government in Italy considered abolishing its Ministry and quickly changed its mind. This is not a viable option.

Option 2. To revive the old Ministry of Food
This would be achieved by separating out food safety and protection tasks from MAFF and, presumably, adding some from the Department of Health (such as nutrition). The resultant Ministry would be small in Whitehall terms and hence would lack 'clout' - as was the case with the Department of Prices and Consumer Protection in the 1970s. In any case, would this new Ministry really be seen as independent of the food industry, even if the sponsorship tasks were located in the Department of Trade and Industry? I do not think it would really help to restore consumer confidence.

Option 3. To transfer MAFF food safety work to the Department of Health

It is here that some of the complex boundary problems in this area start to surface. One could shift MAFF's food safety and science group over to Health. However, the interface between human and animal health is a problem. Would all of animal health be transferred? How would the input of the State Veterinary Service be organised? Would there be sufficient knowledge of food production which is so crucial to food safety? Above all, would shifting responsibility to another Whitehall department, albeit one with a different mission, really reassure the public? This is a better option than 1 and 2 in my view, but not really the answer.

Option 4. To bring in an external food safety chief executive

The proposals recently brought forward seem to be to be a rather weak variant of this combined with Option 5. Such a person could raise the profile of existing food safety work and inject new thinking. They could strengthen and build on the existing food safety advisory structure, but the downside is that they could become the prisoner of that structure. There are certainly limits to what any one person could change, so that this option could be seen as a token public relations gesture likely to have little effect. Much would depend on the person selected for the role.

Option 5. To have an audit body or food policy council

This could come in a variety of forms: one variant is an entity modelled on the National Audit Office which would be accountable directly to Parliament. Most versions of this model see it as encouraging the integration of policy-making; providing an overview of policy and its implementation to safeguard the public interest; and planning a strategy for research policy, including consulting a wider range of experts and using the results of social science research. The role of the Food Safety Council proposed by the Government is seen as being to strengthen the existing network of advisory committees. This would be done by taking a strategic view of the longer-term agenda and identifying issues cutting across the existing network of advisory committees. In other words, it is seen as a supplement to the existing arrangements, rather than a replacement of them. A more general problem with this type of arrangement is how, in practice, it would fit in with the decentralisation of enforcement.

Option 6. The creation of a new food safety agency

This would be responsible for the strategic direction and coordination of food policy and has considerable political and expert support. It may be that only an innovation of this kind would overcome what

David Richardson, writing in *Farmers' Weekly* in February 1997, has described as the false but widespread public perception that farmers, the food trade and MAFF form a cosy cartel which excludes consumers. Organisationally, however, this option poses a number of problems. Careful work would be required on clarifying the lines of responsibility and accountability of the new agency, as well as its tasks and boundaries. The existing network of advisory committees would presumably be brought under its umbrella. Would it be a government department in effect, or would it be seen as a quango which perpetuated the least satisfactory aspects of the old arrangements in a new form? Would it insulate decisions from parliamentary scrutiny, thus making the system less transparent? Have excessive expectations been aroused on the basis of analyses of the United States (US) Food and Drug Administration which fail to take full account of the different constitutional context in which it operates?

THE EUROPEAN DIMENSION
In the light of criticism by the European Parliament on the role of the Commission in the BSE episode, various ideas are under consideration for changes in EU arrangements in relation to food safety. Enforcement is likely to remain essentially a Member State task, but Franz Fischler has called for closer monitoring of Member States' actions by increasing monitoring teams. Jacques Santer has suggested concentrating food safety responsibilities in the consumer affairs directorate in a new food safety agency. Once again the 'I-word' has been heard with calls for an institute of independent scientists to work on animal and public health matters. Santer referred to the US model and it is interesting to note that on January 25th 1997 President Clinton gave three agency heads ninety days to come up with a report on ways of improving the safety of food supply.

CONCLUSION
My view is that underlying all these debates are some quite fundamental value conflicts in society which cannot be resolved by institutional reform. But my brief is to look at the organisational arrangements. Any change is going to involve transition costs and we have to be careful that a new structure does not lead to worse decisions. It seems to me that there is now a critical mass of expectation which demands a different approach. Either one has to have a Food Policy Council on the lines proposed in the Thames Valley University study (Lang *et al* 1996) with a wider remit than that proposed by the government, or one has to have a new Food Safety Agency. But it cannot be independent and it will not achieve as much as some people hope.

REFERENCES

Lang, T, Millstone, E, Raven, H & Rayner, M (1996) *Modernising UK food policy: the case for reforming the Ministry of Agriculture, Fisheries and Food.* London: Centre for Food Policy.

Richardson, D (1997) *Farmers' Weekly,* 7-13 February, p.72.

DISCUSSION

Mr George Kidd (Cabinet Office Deregulation Unit) sought comments on Ms Neville-Rolfe's first alternative which is do nothing, and questioned also whether there is anything that can be done about public confidence or whether public confidence will return as a matter of course.

Professor Wyn Grant, in reply, said that he cannot be sure that public confidence will return as a matter of course and that if he did think it would return he would not be seriously contemplating any these particular options. He added that transitional costs are inevitably associated with all of these options, and that because the problems stem from conflicts in peoples' values and expectations, and are probably deep-rooted, there can be no certainty that changes in structure will bring resolutions at the end of the day. It may be that as the BSE episode recedes, although no-one really quite knows how long the effects may last, even if no further incidents of a comparable kind occur, there could well be a restoration in consumer confidence. He further commented that where expert and informed opinion, and also the press which often deals with these issues in a rather excitable way, create a mass of expectation and public pressure that something has got to be done by government, the risk is that the outcome could be less satisfactory, in which case the right approach may sometimes be to do nothing. However, he was not sure that this would be possible politically in the current situation, even if as a policy analyst he might think it was the most desirable way to proceed.

Mrs Vera Chaney (Green Network) said that consumers are extremely concerned about the health aspects and considered that the loss of confidence arises from the perception that nothing is being done. She felt that following other food problems, the BSE issue had focused the attention of consumers on how we produce our food, and furthermore, they are not encouraged by prolonged scientific argument or debate about regulatory measures. She was convinced that the 'sit back and do nothing' approach is the last thing that the consumer wants.

Professor Wyn Grant agreed that these are all important examples of the value judgements that need to be taken into account, but it must be recognised that people have differing values which lead them to different conclusions about the sort of action that is necessary. He did not feel it right to conclude that nothing has been done in recent years - there has been new legislation, new directives passed by the EU, and significant efforts at the enforcement level to improve training in relation to food hygiene. The main question is what is going to be done now - is it necessarily a change of structure or is an institutional change really required? Or is a change in policy called for, or a change in the kind of values that underpin policy? He considered that structural change of itself will not satisfy the radical critics of the system, or necessarily reassure consumers; and that whilst some things have been done, it seemed to him as a political scientist that what is going on here is a process of conflict within society about values relating to very fundamental things about animals, about food, about the whole society in which we live, and about our health, with which we are all concerned.

Mr John Fuller (Director of the National Federation of Meat and Food Traders) sought comments on the proposition that whether a new 'agency' is set up or whether control of our supply of food to the public continues under the present system, any group in authority will be judged by the things that go wrong, rather than the things that go right; and that human society being what it is, it will continue to go wrong somewhere.

Professor Wyn Grant broadly accepted the premise of the question which he felt related to the point he had made earlier that there is a risk in this whole debate of creating expectations about what can be achieved by institutional reform. He added that the track record in institutional reform in actually bringing about positive change is not terribly good and the very high transition costs are also a key factor.

Mrs Maeve Robertson (National Federation of Consumer Groups) expressed reservations about a new agency since, whatever organisational form it might take, it would continue to attract blame for any food failure or incident in the future. She felt that a restoration of consumer confidence could more effectively be achieved by appropriate changes of attitude and policy in MAFF; and she was also concerned that the emphasis is being placed entirely on food safety and that insufficient attention is being given to nutrition.

Professor Wyn Grant accepted that issues relating to nutrition and diet are of great public health importance and that they have not to some extent been in the forefront of the current debate about a 'Food Safety Agency'. He regarded the suggestion of a reorientation of priorities within MAFF as a particularly interesting option since he felt that the process of reform and change of emphasis of the Common Agricultural Policy (CAP) that is likely to go forward over the next few years, may of itself have some effect on the issues that are currently under debate and may therefore lead to a change in MAFF's role. He also emphasised that in any event, enforcement is essentially going to continue to be decentralised and therefore it is important to consider the points that were made in the last two papers about what constitutes effective enforcement, since we do at the end of the day depend on what happens at that level to ensure that any problems of food supply, safety and quality are anticipated and dealt with as quickly and effectively as possible.

Ms Annabel Holt (Annabel's Crusade for the Environment) felt that all participants at this conference would benefit from a visit to the Henry Doubleday Association to study the advocated methods of food production having regard to the protection of the finite land area of the UK. She further stressed that if producers and food distribution companies concentrated on organic methods, there need be no worries about the effects of toxins.

Marshall BJ & Miller FA (Eds)(1997) *Management of regulation in the food chain - balancing costs, benefits and effects.* CAS Paper 36. Reading: Centre for Agricultural Strategy.

Open Forum

Professor David Hughes in opening the discussion, recognised that there is, probably inevitably, a divide on food legislation and regulatory issues between consumers and the food industry, and the challenge for all the food chain interests represented at this conference is therefore to find ways of minimising the differences. The problems we now face, due largely to the unfortunate incidents of the last couple of years or so, are of loss of consumer confidence in the effectiveness of our food regulatory system, and misunderstandings that arise, amongst other things, from intensive and continuing media interest in food issues.

He stressed the heavy responsibilities that fall on so many, from the primary producers through to the processors, manufacturers, retailers, and caterers, of ensuring the quality and safety of food products expected by the consumers; and also, the important part consumers must themselves play in the handling and preparation of food in the home. It must, he said, be accepted that food laws, and effective machinery for administering and enforcing them, are essential for the protection of the public and he invited conference participants to address the following questions and debate the issues with a panel of the speakers:

(a)   Is the food law regime more complex and burdensome than is genuinely necessary for effective consumer protection, and to what extent does it impede competitiveness, efficiency and innovation in the industries within the food chain?

(b)   What changes in policies, and economic and legal instruments, are necessary to achieve a workable balance likely to be acceptable to all interests comprising the food chain?

(c)   Is there a case for change in the organisational system for food administration, regulation, and enforcement?

Mr R J Tyler (National Federation of Meat and Food Traders) said that he is concerned about inconsistent enforcement that arises, he believes, because local authorities are not adhering to the principles of the 'home authority' concept. He considered that there is still 'empire building' within the trading standards organisation throughout the country which is wasteful of public money, and also concern about the number of occasions on which enforcement authorities having consulted LACOTS (Local Authorities Coordinating Body on Food and Trading Standards) fail to implement their advice.

Mr Paul Allen (County Trading Standards Officer; European Food Law Association of the UK) explained that following collective representations by the local authority associations some 20 years ago urging action specifically to meet the need for better coordination and information in relation to interpretations of the Trade Descriptions Act, the Consumer Credit Act and other relevant legislation causing difficulties for regulators and those being regulated, The Institute of Trading Standards and the local authority associations established LACOTS in 1978. He considered that the operation of the 'home authority' arrangement under which the problems of a multi-based company, or a company with a nationwide network of outlets, are referred to a single enforcement authority for action within guidelines prescribed by LACOTS, has proved to be nothing less than a very considerable success; and whilst final resolution of problems may ultimately be a matter for the courts, the operation of the LACOTS machinery, and also the work of the Deregulation Unit, provides for effective regulatory action within a more friendly and sympathetic framework.

Ms Lucy Neville-Rolfe (Cabinet Office Deregulation Unit) also regarded LACOTS as a body that is providing a necessary function, and added that she had welcomed the extension of its function to include environmental health as well as trading standards matters, as a very useful innovation. She underlined also the business-friendly enforcement procedures introduced under the Deregulation and Contracting Out Act 1994, and explained the 'green card' procedures, the aim and purpose of which is more fair and consistent enforcement. The operation of the 'minded to' procedure under these new provisions provides the opportunity to make representations and to require an explanation of why enforcement officers want the specified actions to be undertaken; and where it has been used, particularly in the areas of health and safety and by the Environment Agency, the procedure has been welcomed by business.

Mr Nigel Matthews (British Retail Consortium) referred to the enormous changes that have taken place in the structure and attitudes of enforcement over the last 20 years, but felt that there are still major problem areas facing small businesses in particular. He added that whilst the 'home authority' principle does not affect the small business man with single premises in a particular town, the 'green card' procedure is beneficial in alleviating concerns given that at the end of the day, if the regulation or hygiene issue cannot be resolved, then the law has to be applied. So far as large businesses are concerned however, the 'home authority' principle is a huge improvement that has taken virtually all the sting out of enforcement, and his company, which deals with about 300 different local authorities, is able to refer matters of principle and interpretation to the London Borough of Southwark as the 'home authority', and discuss them on a regular monthly basis.

Mr Noel Wheatley (Food and Drink Federation) agreed that enforcement is a key issue but wished to turn discussion towards consideration of the case for change in arrangements for food safety administration. We must, he said, first and foremost face the fact that everybody who had spoken at the Conference had recognised that there is a problem at present with consumer confidence, and since we are all consumers as well as having other responsibilities in the food sector, it is as Professor Marsh urged in his opening paper, up to us to do everything possible, with humility and acceptance of the fact that scientific knowledge changes, to assure consumers that legislation is based on the best available scientific advice. Secondly, he wished to raise the question of how consumers can be assured that enforcement is adequate. Whilst LACOTS is doing a fine job and has a very good relationship with the Food and Drink Federation, it seems that openness must be brought into the presentational system if consumers are to be reassured that a good job is being done on the enforcement side.

Professor Wyn Grant (University of Warwick) in reply, said that the interesting question is, who do consumers actually trust? The answer, he felt, was that the people they are most likely to trust are the retailers who retain quite a lot of confidence with consumers, and when information is disseminated to them *via* the retailers, as it is in various forms, it is a very acceptable way of receiving information. So the most effective approach may well be to concentrate on the retailers to rebuild consumer confidence, since it is after all in their interest that consumer confidence should be rebuilt. Consumer confidence had, he felt, been badly shaken by the BSE crisis and by other events, and no assurances are possible that such events will not occur in future - restoration of consumer confidence is not therefore an easy matter.

Ms Margaret Murray (Food Law Group) felt that consumers seem to trust the media, particularly television and radio, so possibly something more needs to be done to get the message of improvements in food safety and quality to the general public through cooking and similar programmes - many of which are put out every day.

Professor Wyn Grant expressed some reservations about this approach since very few journalists have a good understanding of science and he foresaw the risk of these complex and sensitive issues being dealt with in a rather irresponsible way.

Mr Paul Allen suggested that those involved in the current debate about the future structure of food law administration and enforcement might usefully look back to the 1960s/70s when, despite consumer objections, the Consumer Council was abolished by the Government and its functions were taken over by the Office of Fair Trading set up under the Fair Trading Act 1973. The new regime nevertheless recognised the importance of consumer confidence and, to a very considerable extent, placed its trust in the media to communicate information to the public. So, in the context of the problems of the late 1990s, he stressed that whatever structure comes into being, the key will be the establishment of effective communication with consumers, representatives of the consumers, and the media.

Ms Lucy Neville-Rolfe agreed with Mr Noel Wheatley about the need for more openness, and saw this as part of the more general issue of 'risk communication' which would undoubtedly be one of the important areas to be addressed by any new 'agency' or 'council' that may be set up. She also referred to academic studies which include the identification of 'fright factors', where 'risk analysis' experts are working with experts in 'social sciences', a combination likely to be of great interest and significance in developing better understandings and moving the 'risk communications' concept forward.

Mrs Vera Chaney (Green Network) commented that consumer confidence has been lost in the past partly because, in rural areas especially, regulatory officers are 'natives' and too familiar with the people and the businesses in their areas. She advocated greater mobility of enforcement officials which she felt would be more effective and likely to increase confidence within local communities.

Mr John Corbet Milward (Wine and Spirit Association) felt it would be helpful to outline a contingency plan for communications developed by his Association with the media and scientists at some cost and effort, under which a series of simplified briefs had been prepared to explain to journalists the nature of the various problems that might occur in the wine and spirit sector and the likely impact on consumers. Under this plan, the Association is able to trigger a rapid response, and also to isolate problems, in ways that were hitherto not possible.

Mrs Diana Amor (Reading Scientific Services) sought enlightenment on the issue of 'lost confidence' and asked whether this means that consumers are staying in their houses on Saturday mornings instead of going to their usual food supermarkets.

Mr Nigel Matthews said in reply that of the organisations involved in the food chain, the retailers are regarded by the consumer as points of regular contact and reference. As a trade they put out a great deal of information on a wide variety of food issues, as a result of which consumer trust and confidence are being maintained. He instanced his own company's practice of operating a customer care line, carefully monitoring the questions that are raised and trying to provide good answers in a genuine attempt to improve customers' information about products. He also referred to the difficulties of finding the right balance in product labelling since the more information you pack on the label, the less you communicate; and to the importance of information provided to consumers by other means such as through product packaging and cookery programmes.

Mr Colin Andrews (Catering Industry Liaison Council) added that the success of catering businesses depends entirely on consumer confidence - if any catering establishment or restaurant loses the confidence of its customers it is very soon empty and very soon not there at all.

Mrs Joanna Wheatley (Farmer) felt that a key factor in the loss of consumer confidence is the increase in neurological disease, cancers, asthma and respiratory problems which were not so evident in earlier generations and, which she observed, coincides with the industrialisation of agriculture and the introduction of new 'man-made' materials. She therefore urged more intensive monitoring and surveillance by the Department of Health, and by other departments and local authority services concerned with food standards and quality, which would significantly improve the amount and the nature of information available to the scientists.

Dr Spencer Henson (University of Reading) said that he finds the debate about consumer confidence disconcerting in the sense that he sees little evidence of uncertainty or reluctance about food shopping.

He therefore has reservations about assertions that public confidence is at a low level. However, the public does, he felt, have a dilemma in determining how best to react to newspaper headlines warning of a food-health risk against a background of generally sensational journalism. A central aim of the future must be more effective communication so that consumers understand that issues have to be decided on the balances of risk, uncertainties, probabilities and costs, and that science, however good, is not necessarily going to provide single answers. It would furthermore be wrong he added to judge the case for a new 'agency' on the occurrence of further food-related incidents. The success of the responsible authority, whatever its form, must be whether it makes sensible decisions which are communicated to the members of the general public, who are generally capable of understanding and taking account in a rational way of all the benefits, costs, and scientific factors and their interactions.

Mrs Maeve Robertson (MAFF Consumer Panel) took the view that consumers do not generally take media stories very seriously except perhaps the ones that massage the prejudices they already have, but they do trust the retailers. She felt that there is a greater need for a new Freedom of Information Act than for a new 'agency' because consumers do become, not unreasonably, concerned when they hear about a food scare, but cannot find out who or what is perpetrating it. More openness would, she said, restore consumer confidence more than anything else, and the main attraction of the United States Food and Drugs Administration (FDA) system is that it is possible for the public to request and readily receive information.

Dr Spencer Henson commented that, whilst he favoured a greater openness and freedom of information, there must also be a maturity in the way in which it is reported and in the way in which it is received and interpreted by the public generally. If, for example, under a more open system, the initial findings of scientific progress are publicised, there could be an unjustified food scare so more education in the nature of science would need to accompany more freedom of information.

Dr Jack Done (University of Exeter) a veterinary pathologist and epidemiologist, felt that whilst the news media do generate confusion and accelerate its spread, there is also a corporate contribution to misunderstanding from the general population through failure to appreciate properly what is meant by 'scientist'. Considerable problems can arise when scientists in related fields articulate on subjects on which they are not expert. A neurosurgeon, a pathologist or a microbiologist might easily and inadvertently mislead the public about the epidemiology of a transmissible nervous disease like BSE, for example. Furthermore, the world comprises not only the numerate but also the non-numerate. And if people in the latter category do not comprehend 'standard error of the mean', how do they go about deciding whether two or more population groups are different or whether the results of an experiment are significant? A purely subjective opinion of a 'scientist', however eminent, can never be as good as an objective assessment arrived at in a scientific way *via* the appropriate discipline. As a community, we all contribute to confusion through sub-literacy, sub-numeracy and through misuse of terms and concepts.

Mrs Ruth Kirk-Wilson (Meat and Livestock Commission) said that she had been involved in a number of food scares in the past which had necessitated explanation to the public, but she felt that the BSE and *Escherichia coli* cases are quite unique, partly because no precise and authoritative information can yet be given on the basic causal factors and partly because assessments of the degree of risk to health changes as more information becomes available. It was, she felt, particularly difficult to have to explain to people complaining about the lateness of actions on the part of government, that whilst it appears that decisions are generally taken in the light of information available at the time, this may subsequently be found to be insufficient. She also expressed concern that when an attempt was made to encourage food companies to return to the use of British beef by explaining the tightening of controls and regulations by government, it was disappointing that the news media did not regard the story as sufficiently newsworthy.

Mr Paul Allen also saw BSE and *E. coli* as cases of extreme difficulty in terms of communication and public understanding and he instanced as a broad parallel the Chernobyl nuclear incident where enforcement officers in the field were seriously handicapped initially by the lack of information on policy and scientific developments in a fast-moving situation.

Mr George Douglas (Farmer) commenting on behalf of food producers said that he is looking forward to feeding a world population which we are told is going to increase by 50% in the next 15 to 25 years and, if that is the challenge, the only way forward is to make enormous increases in yield. What has happened in the last ten years, however, is that an enormous increase has occurred in the yield of the materials that are wrapped around food in the form of impenetrable packaging. He recalled being told by a very eminent surgeon as long ago as the 1930s that you have got to eat a peck of dirt before you die, so maybe there is something to be said for the argument heard earlier that we are damaging our immune systems by getting things too clean.

Ms Annabel Holt (Annabel's Crusade for the Environment) wished to refer again to the difficulties of buying organic food and urged the representatives of manufacturers and retailers present to meet the demand to reduce the amount of labelling and packaging, and encourage the purchasers of organic food to take away their produce in their own baskets.

Mr Nigel Matthews acknowledged the points made and offered to explain his own company's policy and marketing arrangements for organic food after the conference.

Dr Rod Morrod (Zeneca Agrochemicals) supported the comments made by earlier speakers, and also by Mrs Angela Browning, that there is a need for more public education and understanding of risk perception, risk assessment and risk management in the context of food hygiene. He felt that effective communication between scientists and consumers is of great importance in a technological society but presents a problem because the former do not always have the respect and understanding of the latter, and he sought views on how best to develop the uphill battle of educating the public so that they are not reliant on the media as the major source of information.

Professor Wyn Grant, in reply, said that a change of approach is needed to ensure that the findings of social science research including risk assessment, are incorporated much more into the decision-making process and communicated more effectively to the general public. This might, he felt, be an appropriate role for the envisaged food safety council to become more closely involved in research, and ensure, for example, in the interest of consumer reassurance, that the alternative hypotheses on the origins of BSE and how it was originally transmitted, are not only investigated but communicated to consumers. The whole research agenda should, he felt, be reviewed with the important objective of improving the interface between technology and social science.

Ms Lucy Neville-Rolfe agreed that public understanding of science and technology could well be a top agenda item for a new food safety council and added that the government is doing more work on risk communication which will feed through and change the way that the regulatory agencies behave. She also saw scope for including an appreciation of these issues in the education system and had been impressed by the work of the Environment Agency in providing information packs for schools.

Mr Paul Allen also supported the concept of education of the younger generations and instanced the scheme introduced ten years ago by the

Institute of Trading Standards, which now has a European dimension, of running a 'young consumer of the year' competition.

Ms Margaret Murray proposed more use of the internet system as an increasingly effective method of getting information across to the public in their own homes.

Professor Bevan Moseley (Advisory Committee on Novel Foods Processes and Advisory Committee on Releases into the Environment) referred to Department of Health studies of quantitative risk assessment for microbial infections both food-borne and otherwise which included the proposal that a 'Richter scale of risk' in which all risks were overlaid including gross estimates for food risk from say microbial infections may be the way to achieve public understanding. This would, he felt, register quite low on the 'Richter' scale but would give some indication of the degree of risk in certain foods relative to all other kinds of risks.

Dr Spencer Henson commented that the ways in which scientists judge risk are absolutely fine in terms of scientific investigation and numeracy or sub-numeracy, but the problem is that to consumers it is not just the probabilities that matter, it is the wide range of other effects which have been described as 'fright factors'. Whilst researchers are gradually beginning to understand how consumers perceive risks, the issues are incredibly complex, and currently throw up more research questions than answers.

Mr Charles Cockbill (Chairman of the European Food Law Association of the UK) referred to the range of alternative organisational structures reviewed by Professor Wyn Grant and asked whether, if we had had in place during the last few years, a different structure of decision making, such as the one now favoured by the government, any of the significant food-policy decisions would have been different.

Professor Wyn Grant did not think many of them would have been very different since, at the end of the day, it is not so much a question of structure as a question of policy. In his view the structure would not have prevented the BSE incident or some of the other problems that we have encountered; **Mr Nigel Matthews** suspected that the decisions would not have been that much different but felt that the nature of the publicity might well have brought more resources to the issue at the appropriate stages; **Ms Margaret Murray** felt that perhaps a more inter-disciplinary approach between doctors, scientists and even lawyers looking at the issues might have resulted in more effective and timely understanding and action during the BSE incident.

The Chairman expressed appreciation to conference participants and to the panel of speakers for raising and constructively debating the wide range of issues relating to food regulatory and organisational matters, all of which will be publicised and communicated to the appropriate authorities as soon as possible in the conference proceedings.

Marshall BJ & Miller FA (Eds)(1997) *Management of regulation in the food chain - balancing costs, benefits and effects.*
CAS Paper 36. Reading: Centre for Agricultural Strategy.

Summary and Conclusions

John Marsh

In bringing this conference to its conclusion, may I start with two matters of timing that have concerned me. The first is the timing of this particular event. Would we come to the market at a time when all the interest had disappeared? - I was most reassured that the Minister felt we had not. The second question of timing concerns the gap between you and your tea. I do not propose to keep you for too long.

My first and very pleasant duty is to thank all those who have taken part. We are most grateful to the Minister for her support, to the representatives of consumers and the key sectors of the industry, to fellow academics, and to the team of legal, administrative, and enforcement experts who have contributed richly to our debate today. Not least, I am grateful to our Chairmen. Their continuing contribution to the Centre for Agricultural Strategy (CAS) is very much valued. In a variety of ways they do much to help CAS succeed. When they took on this job, I feared it might be a particularly difficult task. In fact you have been a very well-behaved audience and for that too I am grateful. Finally, may I voice my own thanks for the unfailing support of CAS staff and particularly Bernard Marshall, whose vision and efforts have steered this conference from its earliest conception. It is to him that we must give credit for the very wide range of support and sponsorship which we have received. For this we are indeed most grateful.

This will be the last conference in which I shall take part as a Director of CAS and I am particularly glad that my successor in that role, Dr David Hallam, is with us. One opinion expressed in today's proceedings, which I thought was singularly suitable, was that 'experience is badly overrated'.

I will not in these concluding comments attempt to mention the thirteen papers you have listened to and debated today. Instead I would like to draw your attention to the subtitle of the conference - 'balancing costs, benefits and effects', because in many ways I think the issues we face, are essentially of balance.

From the outset, it was quite clear that if this conference was to succeed it would be necessary to involve many, very complex, and sometimes competing, interests, because all are enmeshed in regulations relating to the food chain. As we have been told several times, it is not just a question of food safety; there are many other regulatory issues which are important - transport, welfare, nutrition and so on. As a result we had to have a large number of contributors. I am most grateful to them all for keeping so well to time.

My first extended contact with this set of issues was as a member of the 1993 Food, Drink and Agriculture Task Force which had been given the task of framing proposals for deregulation. It is interesting that many of the same issues raised by the Task Force have been debated yet again today. Clearly everybody involved wanted food to be safe and, in particular, they wanted it to be known to be safe. They recognised that perceived failures of food safety had very high costs for all involved. They knew, too, that it was difficult to make sure that food was safe because the processes by which food is produced undergo constant change. Traditional rules which once sufficed do not necessarily assure safety. Members of that Task Force wanted the people who buy their food to be able to make informed choices, although there were then, and still are, differences about how that might best be secured. We have too, to remember that the habits of consumers are changing. We live in a society in which, as we have been reminded, values change. What consumers expect from their food and what they are prepared to tolerate in the way in which that food is produced, is different. In such a world, enabling consumers to make informed choices becomes increasingly difficult. The one thing which none of us wants is an industry which tolerates deception in that process.

The Task Force were concerned that the whole industry should be protected from 'the black sheep'. They, the industry, the Ministry, and the local authorities who enforce the regulatory measures, all felt themselves to be vulnerable if things went wrong. So success in food safety and accurate useable information was really important to them all. As we have heard this afternoon, the industry needed then, and still needs, a system which is proportionate and workable. If the rules were not proportionate or workable, they would neither be accepted nor operable. In the Task Force's review, several years ago, we were concerned to make regulations 'goal based' rather than 'prescriptive'. It has been stimulating several years later to re-examine these issues and discover what progress we have made. At the same time it is clear that many of the themes of that debate remain of major concern.

The most notable characteristic of the immediate situation is the urgency, as well as the real sadness, of what has happened in relation to the calamity of Bovine Spongiform Encephalopathy (BSE). It is a calamity. It is a calamity to farmers, to the people who trade in meat, and to the Treasury, whose costs no doubt, we shall all pay. It is a calamity too for consumers, who may well have lost the opportunity to eat products which they would have enjoyed and which were safe. However, the biggest calamity has been a loss of confidence in our food regulatory system, amongst consumers. I listened with great interest to what has been said about the question of how low confidence has really fallen; about whether debate among professionals in the business, and reports in the media, who do have an interest in selling a story, may both undermine confidence and exaggerate its loss. In this conference we have rightly been attentive to the various ways in which the government, the food chain industries, the academics, the lawyers and the enforcement authorities consider that the situation might be improved.

It all comes back to the question of finding an acceptable balance. A balance between risks which we are prepared to live with, and those we feel we should not be asked to live with; a balance between detailed control and intervention in what businesses do, and a system which allows for reasonable innovation and general freedom of action by individuals in business and elsewhere; a balance between the responsibilities which have to be carried by the state and the responsibilities which are those of local enforcement agencies and of the industry itself; a balance between the regulation which is appropriate for the large concern whose products reach every home in the country and for the tiny business which may confine its sales within a very small area. We need too a balance between the means of enforcement. Do we rely on prosecution, or do we emphasise advice and cooperation between the enforcer and the enforced? We need a balance between the economic and legal instruments which we use if society is to attain the food industry it seeks and can afford. We also need a political balance. We cannot in our society have a system of regulation which is not perceived as being ethically acceptable by the bulk of our community. If it does not gain acceptance, it will not function.

In this conference we posed a question, and I was grateful to David Hughes for reminding you of it. In simple terms it asks whether, in the light of all we have heard today, you think that in any of these dimensions we have got the balance right? That has to be for you to decide. Whatever system is adopted, it will seem unfair or inadequate to some sections of the community affected. The outcome will depend, not simply on the system, but upon how it is managed and how it copes when, as will inevitably happen, things do go wrong.

How responsible will the government, the press, the critics, and the industry be when there is failure? Will they do what we sometimes suspect they are doing, and seek to shift the blame to someone else, to maximise the failures of others, to use a failure as a lever to increase their influence or to attract a larger audience for their programme. Or will they recognise that, like all balanced systems, things do go wrong, that existing systems do have to be tuned, and that we do have to allow for corrections. That does not mean that we gain by destroying the system. To do so may compound rather than relieve the problem. So the final balance we need is a balance in our reactions. This is a challenge in which all of us are involved, not just to work out a new system which can restore the lost confidence, but also to operate it in a way which will mean that it deserves and receives the confidence of the whole of society, of the industry, and of its administrators, and of its consumers. In other words, a balance in which each one of us must play a part.

Appendix
List of Authors

Mr Paul Allen OBE, County Trading Standards Officer; Honorary Secretary of The European Food Law Association of the United Kingdom, East Sussex County Council, St Anne's Crescent, Lewes, East Sussex BN7 1SW

Mr Colin Andrews, Chairman, Catering Industry Liaison Council, Colin Andrews Associates, 6 Bowes Road, Walton-on-Thames, Surrey KT12 3HS

Mrs Angela Browning MP, Parliamentary Secretary, Ministry of Agriculture, Fisheries and Food, Whitehall Place, London SW1A 2HH.

Professor Wyn Grant, Professor of Politics, Department of Politics and International Studies, The University of Warwick, Coventry CV4 7AG

Dr Spencer Henson, Lecturer, Department of Agricultural and Food Economics, The University of Reading, PO Box 237, Earley Gate, Reading RG6 6AR

Professor John Marsh CBE, Department of Agricultural and Food Economics, The University of Reading and Director of the Centre for Agricultural Strategy, PO Box 236, Earley Gate, Reading RG6 6AT

Mr Nigel Matthews, Chairman of Food and Drink Committee, British Retail Consortium and Group Secretary, J Sainsbury plc, Stamford House, Stamford Street, London SE1 9LL

Ms Sheila McKechnie OBE, Chief Executive, Consumers' Association, 2 Marylebone Road, London NW1 4DF

Ms Margaret Murray, Food Law Group, Murray and Co, Solicitors, 41 Alexandra Road, Wimbledon, London SW19 7JZ

Ms Lucy Neville-Rolfe, Director of the Deregulation Unit, Cabinet Office, Horseguards Road, London SW1P 3AL

Mr Robert Robertson, Chairman of Agriculture Committee, The Federation of Small Businesses, Press and Parliamentary Office, 2 Catherine Place, Westminster, London SW19 7JZ

Dr Geraldine Schofield, Head of Regulatory and External Affairs, Unilever Research, Colworth Laboratory, Colworth House, Sharnbrook, Bedford MK44 1LQ

Mr David Statham, Head of Environmental Protection, Leicester City Council, New Walk Centre, Welford Place, Leicester LE1 6ZG

Mr Guy Walker CBE, President of Food and Drink Federation and Chairman, Van den Bergh Foods Ltd, Brooke House, Manor Royal, Crawley, West Sussex RH10 2RQ

Chairmen

Morning Sessions

Sir John Quicke CBE, DL, Advisory Committee, Centre for Agricultural Strategy, University of Reading.

Afternoon Sessions

Mr Eric Carter CBE, Advisory Commitee, Centre for Agricultural Strategy, University of Reading.

Professor David Hughes, Sainsbury Professor of Agribusiness and Food Marketing, Wye College, University of London.

Centre for Agricultural Strategy

Sponsorship Scheme

The Centre gratefully acknowledges the long-term support under this
scheme of the following organisations:

DowElanco Europe

The Englefield Charitable Trust

The Ernest Cook Trust

Zeneca Agrochemicals

Centre Publications

Reports

1 *Land for agriculture* (1976) £1.50.
2 *Phosphorus: a source for UK agriculture* (1978) £1.75.
3 *Capital for agriculture* (1978)‡
4 *Strategy for the UK dairy industry* (1978) £2.95.
5 *National food policy in the UK* (1979) £2.85.
6 *Strategy for the UK forest industry* (1980)‡
7 *The efficiency of British agriculture* (1980) £2.85.
8 Jollans, JL (Ed) (1985) *The teaching of agricultural marketing in the UK* £6.00.
9 Jollans, JL (1985) *Fertilisers in UK farming* £8.00.
10 Craig, GM, Jollans, JL & Korbey, A (Eds) (1986) *The case for agriculture: an independent assessment* £9.50.
11 Carruthers, SP (Ed) (1986) *Alternative enterprises for agriculture in the UK*‡
12 Carruthers, SP (Ed) (1986) *Land use alternatives for UK agriculture* £3.00.
13 Harrison, Alan & Tranter, RB (1989) *The changing financial structure of farming* £8.75.
14 Harrison, Alan & Tranter, RB (1994) *The recession and farming: crisis or readjustment?* £8.50.
15 Carruthers, SP, Miller, FA & Vaughan, CMA (Eds) (1994) *Crops for industry and energy.* £18.50

Papers

1 Marsh, JS (1977) *UK agricultural policy within the European Community* £1.50.
2 Tranter, RB (Ed) (1978) *The future of upland Britain* Proceedings of a symposium organised by CAS in conjunction with the Department of Agriculture and Horticulture, 19-22 September 1977‡

3   Harrison, A, Tranter, RB & Gibbs, RS (1977) *Landownership by public and semi-public institutions in the UK* £1.75.

4   Collins, EJT (1978) *The economy of upland Britain, 1750-1950: an illustrated review* £2.20.

5   McCalla, AF (1978) *International agricultural research: potential impact on world food markets and on UK agricultural strategy‡*

6   Swinbank, A (1978) *The British interest and the green pound‡*

7   Robbins, CJ (Ed) (1978) *Food, health and farming: reports of panels on the implications for UK agriculture* £2.40.

8   Ritson, C (1980) Self-sufficiency and food security £2.00.

9   Tranter, RB (Ed) (1981) *Smallfarming and the Nation* Proceedings of a conference organised by the Smallfarmers' Association, 27 March 1980 £2.00.

10   Jollans, JL (Ed) (1981) *Grassland in the British economy* Proceedings of a symposium organised by the Department of Agriculture, the Department of Agricultural Economics and Management, the Grassland Research Institute and the Centre for Agricultural Strategy, 15-17 September 1980 £10.00.

11   Marshall, BJ & Tranter, RB (Eds) (1982) *Smallfarming and the rural community* Proceedings of a conference organised by the Smallfarmers' Association, 28 March 1981‡

12   Hallam, D (1983) *Livestock development planning: a quantitative framework‡*

13   Carruthers, SP & Jones, MR (1983) *Biofuel production strategies for UK agriculture* £6.50.

14   Jollans, JL (1983) *Agriculture and human health* Report of a study and the proceedings of a symposium, 11-13 July 1983‡

15   Tranter, RB (Ed) (1983) *Strategies for family-worked farms in the UK* Proceedings of a symposium organised by the Smallfarmers' Association and the Centre for Agricultural Strategy, 21-22 September 1983 £7.50.

16   Korbey, A (Ed) (1984) *Investing in rural harmony: a critique* Proceedings of a seminar organised by the Centre for Agricultural Strategy, 10 April 1984 £5.00.

17   Korbey, A (Ed) (1985) *Food production and our rural environment - the way ahead* Proceedings of a symposium organised by the Centre for Agricultural Strategy, 19 November 1984 £5.50.

18   Miller, FA & Tranter, RB (Eds) (1988) *Public perception of the countryside* Papers presented at a conference organised by the Centre for Agricultural Strategy as part of a study commissioned by the Countryside Foundation, 7 January 1988 £4.50.

19   Bennett, RM (Ed) (1989) *The greenhouse effect and UK agriculture* Proceedings of a conference organised by the Centre for Agricultural Strategy, 14 July 1989 £15.00.

20   Miller, FA (Ed) (1990) *Food safety in the human food chain* Proceedings of a conference organised by the Centre for Agricultural Strategy, 27 September 1989 £15.00.

21 Bather, DM & Miller, FA (1991) *Peatland utilisation in the British Isles* £2.00. (The detailed report to the Peat Producers' Association entitled 'Peatland utilisation in the UK and Ireland', on which Paper 21 is based, is also available)

22 Carruthers, SP (Ed) (1991) *Farm animals: it pays to be humane* Proceedings of a conference organised by the Centre for Agricultural Strategy, 12 September 1990 £15.00.

23 Wise, TE (Ed) (1991) *Agricultural and food research - who benefits?* Proceedings of a conference organised by the Centre for Agricultural Strategy, 18 December 1990 £14.00.

24 Miller, FA (Ed) (1991) *Agricultural policy and the environment* Proceedings of a conference organised by the Centre for Agricultural Strategy, 7 June 1991 £13.50.

25 Marshall, BJ (Ed) (1992) *Sustainable livestock farming into the 21st Century* Proceedings of a conference organised by the Centre for Agricultural Strategy, 12 September 1991 £15.50.

26 CAS (1992) *Strategies for the rural economy* Proceedings of a conference organised by the Centre for Agricultural Strategy, 30 June 1992 £30.00.

27 Miller, FA (Ed) (1993) *Eastern Europe: opportunities and needs for food and agriculture* Proceedings of a conference organised by the Centre for Agricultural Strategy , 17 September 1992 £19.50.

28 Carruthers, SP & Miller, FA (Eds) (1996) *Crisis on the family farm: ethics or economics?* Proceedings of a conference organised by the Centre for Agricultural Strategy and the Small Farmers' Association, 30-31 March 1993 £25.00.

29 Marshall, BJ & Miller, FA (Eds) (1994) *Water services and agriculture: key issues and strategic options* Proceedings of a conference organised by the Centre for Agricultural Strategy, 14 December 1993 £20.00.

30 Ansell, DJ & Vincent, SA (1994) *An evaluation of set-aside management in the European Union with special reference to Denmark, France, Germany and the UK* £22.50.

31 Marshall, BJ & Miller, FA (Eds) (1995) *Priorities for a new century - agriculture, food and rural policies in the European Union* Proceedings of a conference organised by the Centre for Agricultural Strategy, 24 November 1994 £20.00.

32 Jones, PJ, Rehman, T, Harvey, DR, Tranter, RB, Marsh, JS, Bunce, RGH, & Howard, DC (1995) *Developing LUAM (Land Use Allocation Model) and modelling CAP reforms* £16.50.

33 Errington, AJ & Harrison-Mayfield, LE with Jones, PJ (1996) *Modelling the employment effects of changing agricultural policy* £11.00.

34 Marshall, BJ & Miller, FA (Eds) (1996) *Biotechnologies in agriculture and food - coming to the market.* Proceedings of a conference organised by the Centre for Agricultural Strategy, 5 March 1996. £19.50.

35 Thirtle, CG, Piesse, J & Smith, VH (1997) *An economic approach to the structure, historical development and reform of agricultural R&D in the UK* £10.75.

36 Marshall, BJ & Miller, FA (Eds) (1997) *Management of regulation in the food chain - balancing costs, benefits and effects.* Proceedings of a conference organised by the Centre for Agricultural Strategy, 11 February 1997 £15.00.

‡ Out of print but available in facsimile

Joint Publications
2 Choe, ZR (1986) *A Strategy for pasture improvement by smallfarmers in upland Korea* Published in collaboration with Gyeonsang National University, Korea £10.00.
3 Ansell, DJ & Done, JT (1988) *Veterinary research and development: cost benefit studies on products for the control of animal diseases* Published jointly with the British Veterinary Association £5.00.
4 Ansell, DJ & Tranter, RB (1992) *Set-aside; in theory and in practice* Published jointly with the Department of Agricultural Economics and Management, University of Reading £14.50.

Mailing List
To receive notification of all future publications please ask to be put on the mailing list.
Standing Orders
To receive invoiced copies of all future publications please ask to be put on the standing order list.
Orders
All publications available from: The Centre for Agricultural Strategy, University of Reading, PO Box 236, 1 Earley Gate, Reading RG6 6AT. Telephone: 0118 931 8152; Fax: 0118 935 3423; Email: CASGRI@reading.ac.uk. Prices include postage. Please make cheques payable to 'The University of Reading'. We cannot accept payment by 'BACS'.